Grand Central Publishing
Hachette Book Group
1290 Avenue of the Americas, New York, NY 10104
grandcentralpublishing.com
twitter.com/grandcentralpub

First Edition: January 2018

Grand Central Publishing is a division of Hachette Book Group, Inc. The Grand Central Publishing name and logo is a trademark of Hachette Book Group, Inc.

Investigation Discovery and the ID Investigation Discovery logo are trademarks of Discovery Communications, LLC.

The publisher is not responsible for websites (or their content) that are not owned by the publisher.

The Hachette Speakers Bureau provides a wide range of authors for speaking events. To find out more, go to www.hachettespeakersbureau.com or call (866) 376-6591.

Library of Congress Control Number: 2017956662

ISBNs: 978-1-5387-4481-9 (trade paperback), 978-1-5387-4656-1 (hardcover library edition), 978-0-316-51492-7 (ebook)

Printed in the United States of America

LSC-C

10 9 8 7 6 5 4 3 2 1

HOME SWEET MURDER

TRUE-CRIME THRILLERS

JAMES PATTERSON

As Seen on Investigation Discovery's *Murder Is Forever*

GRAND CENTRAL
PUBLISHING

NEW YORK   BOSTON

Dear Reader,

Above all else I'm a storyteller. I craft stories for insatiable readers. And though my books may seem over-the-top to some, I find that I am most often inspired by real life. After all, truth is stranger than fiction.

The crimes in this book are 100% real. Certain elements of the stories, some scenes and dialogue, locations, names, and characters have been fictionalized, but these stories are about real people committing real crimes, with real, horrifying consequences.

And as terrifying and visceral as it is to read about these crimes gone wrong, there's something to remember: the bad guy always gets caught.

If you can't get enough of these true crimes, please watch the pulse-racing new television series on Investigation Discovery, Murder Is Forever, where you'll see these shocking crimes come to life.

I hope you're as haunted by these accounts as I am. They'll remind you that though humans have the capacity for incredible kindness, we also have the capacity for unspeakable violence and depravity.

CONTENTS

HOME SWEET MURDER

CHAPTER 1

LEO FISHER HOLDS A pair of boxer undershorts to the knife wound in his neck, trying to stop the flow of blood pumping out. The shorts don't seem to be doing much good. The fabric is soaked. His arm is slathered in sticky blood.

The sixty-one-year-old tries to take shallow, calming breaths. A spasm of pain rips through his chest. If the gouge in his neck doesn't kill him, under such stress his heart condition surely will.

Hold on! he tells himself. *Stay calm.*

The advice seems impossible considering the circumstances. The house's burglar alarm screams around him, a deafening, maddening tone that seems to grow louder and louder with each peal.

Faintly, from beyond the wail of his house's alarm, he can just make out police sirens, getting closer.

Leo is sitting on the floor, leaning against the wall next to the hallway leading to the bedroom and his office. He doesn't know where his wife is. He had blacked out and was awakened by the siren going off.

"Sue!" he calls, but there is no answer. "Muffy!" he yells again, using his pet name for her.

One of their cats pads down the hall, startling Leo. Its eyes are wild, its hair spiked. It's more than the alarm that spooked it, Leo realizes. The cat is leaving a path of bloody paw prints behind as it runs into the living room.

"Sue," Leo croaks, knowing the blood must belong to his wife of forty years.

The police sirens are suddenly very loud. There is a crashing at the door.

"*Police!*" a voice shouts.

Leo hears footsteps in the foyer.

He musters all the strength he can to yell out in a hoarse, trembling voice, "In here."

A uniformed police officer appears, his gun drawn. Another officer follows close behind.

"My wife," Leo croaks. "Do you see her?"

The first officer drops to his knees to help Leo. The second continues down the hall. Leo cranes his neck to watch the man.

From his angle going down the hallway, the officer can see into the office. A woman lies facedown on the floor next to the desk. The carpet beneath her is a swamp of crimson. Her back appears to be stippled with puncture wounds, with bloodstains blooming like roses through her white sweater.

Her hair is matted with blood.

She isn't moving.

Leo sees the look of horror on the officer's face. That's the last thing Leo is able to take—he passes out. His limp hand falls, pulling away the makeshift bandage that was stemming his blood flow.

Fresh blood pumps out of his neck in rhythm with his heartbeat. Each pulse of blood is weaker than the one before it.

CHAPTER 2

Earlier that night
November 9, 2014
6:00 p.m.

LEO SITS AT THE table, reading a novel, while Sue moves around the kitchen preparing their dinner. They've been married forty years, and this has become their evening ritual: Sue cooking while Leo keeps her company. They have lots of friends and enjoy plenty of social opportunities, but on any particular day, if given the choice, they like to stay home together.

For all the money Leo makes at the law firm, they like a simple life.

Sue notices Leo's empty glass of water and says, "Do you want me to get you a refill, Pie?"

"Pie" is her nickname for him.

"Sure," he says, pushing his glasses up the bridge of his nose.

Sue fills his water glass at the refrigerator and brings it to him. He looks up from the pages to offer her an appreciative smile.

"Thanks, Muffy."

Leo has a kind face. It's one of the things she's always loved about him. She noticed it when he was a twenty-year-old kid with dreams of becoming a lawyer, and she notices it now, four decades later. He's gained a few pounds and most of his hair has fallen out—and what hair is left has turned white—but the kindness behind his smile has never changed.

Sue turns back to the kitchen counter, where she is preparing a basting sauce for their chicken dinner. She pushes the sleeves of her white sweater up to her elbows to make sure she doesn't get anything on them. She combines olive oil, garlic, thyme, sage, salt, and pepper. She pours the mixture over the chicken breasts, then uses tongs to flip the breasts over and coat both sides.

The oven isn't quite preheated yet, so she turns her attention to a few dishes in the sink.

Then she has a thought.

"Pie," she says, trying not to sound like a nag, "did you take your medicine?"

"I will in a minute," Leo says, not looking up from his book.

Sue doesn't say a word. Instead, she leaves the kitchen and walks through the living room toward the hallway leading to the back of the house. Their home is nice—spacious but not extravagant. In McLean, Virginia, there are certainly bigger, more expensive houses. Ten miles from Washington, DC, the suburban community is home to diplomats, businessmen, and high-ranking government officials.

Most of Sue and Leo's income comes from Leo's work as a partner for the Bean, Kinney & Korman law firm in nearby Arlington. He works on cases involving trademarks, copyrights, business transactions, corporate disputes—nothing particularly exciting by most standards, but nevertheless a career that has given them a comfortable life together.

Sue walks down the hallway. She isn't sure where Leo keeps his pills. She checks their bedroom first. She flicks on the light and spots both of their cats, Twist and Shout, submerged in the thick, snow-white duvet covering Sue and Leo's California king bed. Twist raises his head and whips his tail rhythmically while Shout purrs loudly.

"Hi, sweeties," Sue says, running her hands along both cats' soft fur.

On each side of their bed, she and Leo have their own nightstands. Leo's is practically empty except for a lamp and a handful of books in his to-read pile.

No pills.

She doesn't expect his medication to be on her side, but she checks anyway. There is nothing there but her face cream and a landline telephone.

She crosses through the bedroom into the bathroom they share. She checks his medicine cabinet. No luck.

She frowns. *Where are those darn pills?*

She leaves the bedroom and goes into Leo's home office across the hall. Bookshelves line the back wall, filled with a wide variety of fiction and nonfiction titles, and decorated with framed photos and novelties purchased on their travels abroad. There is a love seat against one wall, with a couple throw pillows. A small end table sits to one side with a few more of Leo's books lying on it. Leo's desk, on the opposite wall, is neat and organized, with a large-screen desktop computer, another telephone, and a case file lying open. Sitting on the corner of the desk is a small bottle of prescription medication.

Sue checks the label to verify what it is.

Of course, she thinks. *His heart is in his work, so why not keep his heart medication in his office?*

She snatches the bottle off the surface of the desk and heads back to the kitchen. On her way through the living room, something catches her eye out the front picture window.

A vehicle is parked on the road at the end of their driveway. It's an SUV of some sort, with its interior lights illuminated. She can make out two figures inside but, at this distance, can't discern any details about them.

As if they can sense her watching, the lights inside the car go off, and everything behind the windows turns black.

It's not unusual for people to park on the street in this neighborhood, but the properties are big enough, with long driveways, that people don't often park anywhere but in front of the houses they're visiting.

They must be lost, Sue thinks.

Maybe they stopped to look at a map or their GPS. Or to make a phone call or send a text.

But several seconds pass, and the car doesn't move.

Sue suddenly realizes that they could be watching her,

just as she had been watching them. The ceiling light is on, as well as a lamp in the corner, which would backlight Sue's silhouette and make it easy for anyone on the road to see her standing there.

Sue feels goosebumps rise on her skin and she isn't sure why.

She yanks the curtain closed and heads back toward the kitchen, telling herself there's nothing to worry about.

CHAPTER 3

"HERE YOU GO," SUE says, setting the prescription bottle on the table next to Leo's glass of water.

Leo puts his book down on the table and dutifully takes his pills.

"Is this how you're going to spend your retirement, Muffy?" he says, taking a good-humored, teasing tone. "Keeping track of what I'm supposed to be doing?"

"If you would just retire too," Sue says, returning to the counter and her dinner preparations, "then you could keep track of yourself."

Leo chuckles. This is an ongoing conversation these days. Sue recently retired from a career in finance, and she's been pressing him to join her.

"I'm only sixty-one—not ninety-nine," Leo says. "I'm not ready to retire. I know it's what was right for you, but it's not for me. Not yet."

"People don't have quadruple bypass surgeries just to sit behind a desk," Sue says, using a spoon to ladle more sauce onto the chicken breasts.

"I love what I do," Leo says.

"Oh, I know," she teases. "I'm well aware of your undying affair with the firm."

Leo laughs and picks his book back up. If her jibes made any dent, he doesn't show it.

She wishes he'd take her concerns seriously. She's been thinking about mortality—both of theirs—ever since he had the heart attack that led to the surgery. They are both sixty-one, which isn't old, but they aren't spring chickens anymore.

It isn't that she thinks they need to spend every minute of their lives together. But he works too hard. Even after his heart attack, Leo seems to think he will live forever. She can't help but worry about him.

She can't imagine life without him.

The oven buzzes, signaling that the preheat temperature has been reached. Sue opens the door, and, as she puts the casserole dish inside, the heat of the oven fogs the edges of her glasses.

She sets the timer and says, "Okay, dinner will be ready in—"

The doorbell rings.

Leo looks up from his book. Sue frowns and shrugs her shoulders, telling him she doesn't know who it could be.

"Probably the courier from the firm," Leo says, setting his book down and rising from his chair.

"On a Sunday night?" Sue says. "Are you expecting anything?"

"Not that I can think of," Leo says.

He seems to think nothing of it, but Sue can't help but find it odd that Leo would be receiving files over the weekend without even knowing that they're coming.

Is he so busy that he can't even keep track of what files are supposed to be delivered?

"Can't we have one night to ourselves without your job interrupting us?"

Sue intends the question to be a tease, like the tone he used with her earlier, but when the words come out, she doesn't recognize her own voice. She sounds like the nag she doesn't want to be.

"I'm sure it's nothing," Leo says, seeming not to notice.

As Leo walks toward the foyer to answer the door, Sue remembers the car parked in front of their house. She opens her mouth to tell him to wait, but he's already out of the room. Besides, what would she say? *There's a strange car parked on the street?* So what. This isn't a gated community. Anyone can drive down the street and park in front of their house.

Anyone.

The bell rings again.

CHAPTER 4

THE MAN AT THE door clearly isn't a courier from the office. He is wearing a suit, but the fabric is wrinkled, as if he's been sleeping in his clothes. Atop his head is a brown fedora like Harrison Ford wore in the Indiana Jones movies.

The man pulls a badge from his jacket, flashes it in front of Leo's face, then makes it disappear back into his suit.

"I'm Jeffrey Wilkins from the SEC," the man says. "I need to come in and ask you some questions."

"I don't understand," Leo says, trying to make sense of what is happening. "What is this about?"

"Sir," the agent says, "it's urgent that I come inside."

The agent tries to step forward, but Leo doesn't make room for him. The man stands uncomfortably close to Leo.

"Are you sure you have the right address? My name is Leo Fisher."

"Time is of the essence. We're investigating misconduct at your firm, and I need to ask you a few questions. We're speaking with all the partners. I've just come from Mr. Korman's residence."

"On a Sunday night?" Leo says.

"Like I said, this is urgent."

Leo's heart starts to race. *What is going on?*

"I'm not at liberty to discuss matters relating to my firm," Leo says. "Or my clients."

"Even when something illegal is going on?"

"There is nothing illegal going on at the firm," Leo says.

"You're sure?"

"To my knowledge, yes."

The agent is probably in his thirties, but he has a chubby, boyish face, with a brown goatee and a sorry excuse for a mustache. Despite his youthful features, there is something in the man's face that is disquieting. Anger seems to be bubbling just beneath the surface.

"I'm sorry, but I'm going to have to ask you to leave," Leo says. "If you want to drop by the office tomorrow, I'd be happy to speak with you."

"Really?"

"Yes."

"If I come tomorrow," the agent says, "I'm bringing a warrant—and police. I think it would be easier if we talk tonight. Off the record."

Leo thinks for a moment.

"May I see that badge again?" Leo asks.

Leo expects the agent to oblige and show his badge, even if he is irritated by the request. But the agent does nothing of the sort.

Instead, he shoves Leo—hard—in the chest.

Leo stumbles back into the foyer. The man steps into the house and swings the door shut behind him. He throws the deadbolt.

Leo stares in disbelief.

Sue walks in from the kitchen, wiping her hands on a towel.

"What's going on?" she says.

"Ma'am," the agent says with authority. "I'm with the Securities Exchange Commission. I have some questions for your husband."

"Leo?" Sue says, turning to her husband. "I don't understand."

Leo can't bear the look of confusion and fear on his wife's face. This isn't right.

"This is unacceptable," Leo says to the agent. "I know the law. I know my rights. You need to leave."

"You're the one who did something unacceptable," the agent snaps. "And you're going to be in even more trouble if you don't cooperate."

"I demand to see your identification," Leo says.

The man takes a deep breath, like a parent dealing with a petulant child. He reaches into his jacket. But he doesn't pull out his credentials. He pulls out what looks like a toy gun from a science fiction movie.

The agent points the object at Leo, and in the instant before the man squeezes the trigger, Leo realizes what it is.

CHAPTER 5

TWO BARBED ELECTRODES SHOOT from the gun and stab into Leo's sweater. Lightning bolts of pain explode through his body. The electricity blasting through him paralyzes his muscle function, and he drops to the ground, convulsing.

The pain is extraordinary—every bit as excruciating as his heart attack. Leo fears he is having another heart attack, but then the electricity cuts off and the pain begins to subside.

He is a useless blob of jelly lying on his foyer floor, but he knows he is going to live. Unless, that is, his assailant decides to zap him with the Taser gun again. Leo isn't sure he can survive another shock.

Faintly, over his own garbled moans of pain, Leo can hear his wife screaming.

"You can't do this!" Sue shouts. "This is outrageous."

The agent ignores her and crouches over Leo, fastening his hands and ankles with zip ties. The agent disconnects and retracts the cords from the Taser.

Sue stands frozen, unsure what to do. Finally, her paralysis breaks, and she steps forward to help Leo.

The man cuts her off before she makes it two steps.

"Don't move," he says. "I'll zap you too, you bitch!"

He grabs her arm and shoves her against the wall. He is much stronger than she is, and he holds her arms together then encircles her wrists with a zip tie. The plastic strips cut into her skin. He fastens her ankles together. Sue tries to bring her breathing under control and to keep herself from crying.

The man leaves the two of them there—Leo lying on the floor, Sue precariously balanced on zip-tied legs—and starts closing the blinds in the front-facing rooms.

"Pie," Sue says, her voice barely more than a whisper. "Are you okay?"

"I'm okay," Leo says, but this is far from true.

His limbs feel like Jell-O, and his muscles ache. It's as if every muscle in his body had seized up with charley horses, and only now are the muscles beginning to loosen. Worse, he feels a painful squeezing in his chest. Not a heart attack—not yet—but it's serious enough that, under normal circumstances, he would lie down and try to relax.

Relaxing is impossible right now.

"What's this about, Pie?" Sue says. "What kind of trouble are we in?"

"I don't know."

This statement seems to enrage the agent, who storms back into the room.

"You don't know?" he says, kneeling over Leo and practically shouting in his face. "We'll see about that."

The agent leans over and jerks Leo to sit upright. The man winces and reaches for his lower back.

"Get up and go to the bedroom," the agent says, holding his back like he just strained a muscle.

Leo and Sue hobble down the hallway. From their bedroom door, Twist and Shout watch them suspiciously. As if they can tell something is wrong, the cats take off running.

The agent makes Leo and Sue sit on the edge of their bed.

"Let's get this interrogation started," the agent says.

CHAPTER 6

A CHAIR SITS IN the corner with a small pile of Leo's unfolded clothes. The agent brushes the clothes out of the chair and eases down onto its cushion as if the act of sitting is difficult. He takes off his hat and sets it on the floor. His hair is disheveled and flattened on one side from the fedora. His forehead is beaded with sweat.

He reaches into his pants pocket and pulls out a prescription bottle. He pops a tiny pill into his mouth and swallows.

"This is outrageous," Leo says. "This is a clear violation of our civil rights."

The agent rises from his chair and looms over Leo and Sue.

"You'd be advised not to make this any more difficult than it has to be, Mr. Fisher. You know what you've done."

Sue's eyes widen, looking at Leo for answers.

He shrugs, a gesture meant to say he doesn't have any.

The agent begins to pace back and forth in front of them like a cop on a TV show.

Sue has a strange surreal feeling—like she's somehow been teleported from her normal life and dropped into an episode of *The Twilight Zone*.

This is our bedroom, she thinks. *In our home!*

And we're being questioned in it like criminals!

"Leo Fisher, managing partner at Bean, Kinney & Korman," the agent says, as much to himself as Leo. "And you've been there since 1990? Is that right?"

Leo nods, and the agent turns his attention to Sue.

"And you're recently retired, isn't that right, Susan? Enjoying the life of a housewife, are we?"

Sue glares at him. What kind of questions are these? What does her retirement have to do with Leo's law firm?

"Will you just tell us what this is about already?" Sue says.

The agent glares at her. She feels like squirming under his gaze, but she holds her head high and does not look away.

"What this is about," the agent says, "is some very irregular activity at the firm in the past month."

"Irregular activity?" Leo says.

"Don't interrupt," the agent snaps, then turns his attention back to Sue.

"There are hints of very dubious wire transfers at your husband's direction," the man says. "And intercepted emails to prove it."

"This must be a mistake," Leo says.

"It's no mistake, I'm afraid," the agent said. "Either you're up to no good, or someone in the firm is framing you. Now I need some answers."

The agent peels off his jacket and tosses it on the chair in the corner. Without the jacket, they can see the Taser fastened to the man's belt, as well as a shoulder holster containing what looks like a semi-automatic pistol.

Do SEC agents carry firearms? Sue wonders.

The agent starts bombarding Leo with questions about any illicit activities at the firm. Shady employees who might be framing him? Clients who have criminal histories? Offshore accounts?

"I don't know about anything like that," Leo says. "Can you be more specific? Our firm deals in commercial and civil litigation. We have a high standard for clients we'll work with—there's nothing duplicitous going on."

"So that's the way you want to play it, huh?" the agent says, shaking his head.

"Play what?"

"You know what I'm talking about," the agent snaps. "Stop acting as if you're innocent."

The agent runs his hand through his hair, and his expression changes. For an instant, he lets his guard down. Instead of looking like a confident—and angry—government agent, he suddenly looks different. He looks like an ordinary guy. Someone you might pass on the street or in a hallway.

Imagining him this way—in another context, wearing different clothes—Leo thinks for a moment that he might know the man. There is just a glimmer of recognition, but then the agent's bad-tempered expression is back.

Leo turns away, not wanting his own expression to reveal his speculation. Leo is sure now that he's seen the man somewhere before.

But where?

CHAPTER 7

Two weeks earlier

LEO IS SITTING IN his office at Bean, Kinney & Korman, leaning over a case file. Sunlight pours into the office from a floor-to-ceiling window at Leo's back. Outside, the trees are ablaze with fall colors.

Leo's office is large, spacious, and spotless. Leo's diplomas hang on the wall: a bachelor's degree from Oberlin College in 1975 and his law degree from George Washington University in 1980. There is also a plaque denoting Leo as one of the "Best Lawyers in America in Commercial Litigation."

On Leo's expansive desk is a new twenty-seven-inch iMac computer, flanked by two framed photographs. One photo is a recent one, taken of Leo and Sue on the beach during a vacation in Turks and Caicos. There is also an older photo of the two of them standing in front of the Berlin Wall during a trip to Germany in the 1980s. The Wall is covered in graffiti, and the two posed for the pic under a place where someone had painted, "They came, they saw, they did a little shopping!" Leo still had most of his hair in the photo—and it hadn't turned white yet.

Nearly thirty years has passed since the picture was taken. While Leo's offices have grown over the years—as has his paycheck—his work ethic has not waned. He is reading this case file with the same vigor he did when he was a young lawyer still trying to make a name for himself in corporate law.

There is a gentle knock on the door, and a blurred face appears behind the textured glass of the door's window. Without looking up, Leo says, "Come in."

Phil Yeager, another partner at the firm, pokes his head into the office.

"You ready, Leo?" he says.

Leo stares blankly at his silver-haired friend, then his eyes open and his mouth becomes an O.

"The meeting!" Leo says. "I almost forgot."

Phil laughs.

"Almost forgot? You did forget."

Leo, embarrassed, gets to his feet, checks his watch, sees that he's even more late than he thought, and heads toward the door. Only then does he realize that he needs his notes, and he heads back to his desk.

Phil is grinning. He isn't upset by the tardiness, just amused. They walk down the hall together, passing cubicles of lawyers reading through large stacks of case files, talking on the phone with clients, and writing briefs on desktop computers. As the two partners walk through the workspace in their three-piece Hugo Boss suits, most of the lawyers look up as they pass, saying hello or nodding a greeting.

As they pass one desk in particular, a pretty dark-haired woman looks up from a manila folder thick with court transcripts. Phil does not make eye contact. He keeps his head facing forward, like he's ignoring a homeless person panhandling for change at a stoplight.

Leo doesn't ignore the woman. He nods at her and smiles.

"Hi, Alecia," he says.

"Hi, Leo," says the woman, who has a chubby face and a bright smile.

When Leo and Phil arrive to the conference room, the other partners jibe Leo for being late, though no one actually seems upset. Life is good at the law firm of Bean, Kinney & Korman.

Leo stands before the group and begins his presentation. Leo's job today is to give the partners a summary of their third quarter: both the cases that are being litigated as well as the company's financial picture.

All is good, and the partners react with smiles, laughs, and jokes.

Just as the meeting is wrapping up, Phil raises his hand and says, "Leo, I hate to end things on a sour note, but you didn't mention our bit of unpleasant business. What are you going to do about our little problem?" He draws out the two syllables of the word "problem" and makes a face as he says it—as if the word itself is uncomfortable to utter.

"Well," Leo says. "I don't know if I'd call it a 'problem.'"

"Oh, I would," another partner, Bill, pipes up. "This could damage the reputation of the firm if it's not cleaned up quickly."

"And quietly," someone adds.

"We need to take action for the good of the firm," says Jennifer, one of the newest lawyers to be promoted to partner. "We've let this go on too long now already."

"It's a little problem right now," says Phil, "but it could be a big one if we don't nip it in the bud—if you know what I mean," he adds.

Leo does know what he means. Unfortunately, Leo also knows that the responsibility for dealing with the "problem" is going to fall on him.

As much as he loves his job, this is a part he doesn't like.

"I'll take care of it," Leo says.

CHAPTER 8

THE AGENT ASKS LEO to think hard about what was happening at the firm in October.

"In October?" Leo says. "You mean last month?"

"Yes, last month," the agent snaps.

Sue watches Leo out of the corner of her eye. He has a perplexed look on his face. Either he doesn't have any idea what the agent is talking about or he's a very good actor.

Sue has only ever known Leo to be a devoted husband—a good, genuine man. She fell in love with his kind smile and has never known him to be anything but the gentle man she fell for all those years ago. But she hasn't spent much time with him when he's in his work environment. Not in the office. Not in the courtroom. Maybe he's good at putting up a front and she doesn't know it.

"Okay," Leo says. "October. Let's see. We've been hired to help a startup company develop non-compete clauses for its employees. We're working with a real-estate developer on some land-use ordinances. And we've been busy with a trademark infringement case in federal court."

He says the last one like it's a question. Could this be the case the agent is referring to?

The agent shakes his head. His cheeks are flushed with anger and frustration.

Sue has had enough of this back-and-forth.

"This isn't the time to be protecting someone, honey," she says to Leo. "Just tell the truth."

Leo shrugs his shoulders and frowns, looking genuinely bewildered.

"I honestly don't know what he's asking for," Leo says. "Nothing out of the ordinary happened at the firm in the time frame he's referring to."

The agent leans over and pokes a finger into Leo's chest.

"You've got a really lousy memory," the agent barks.

He begins pacing again. Sue notices that he is wearing black gym shoes, which are well-worn and scuffed, with Velcro instead of laces. They look dirty, and this makes her wince because the carpet in this part of the house is plush and ivory-colored. It stains easily, and therefore Sue and Leo usually take their shoes off in the bedroom. This man with old dirty shoes is tromping all over their expensive white carpet.

The appearance of the shoes strikes her as odd. She lets her eyes drift up to examine the agent, really paying attention to his appearance for the first time. His suit is wrinkled, and the fabric looks cheap. She doesn't imagine an agent of the SEC would necessarily wear the type of expensive suits and shoes that Leo can afford, but she thinks the man would want to look more professional than he does.

She looks at his tie and then at the fedora on the floor and jacket on the chair. None of the ensemble matches. Even if the guy has no fashion sense, she thinks, any employee at Men's Wearhouse could help him pick out a relatively affordable matching suit, tie, and pair of dress shoes.

Now that she looks at him, the face doesn't match the clothes either. His chunky cheeks, thin goatee, and peach-fuzz mustache make him look like a frat boy wearing a costume for some kind of college prank.

His outfit looks like something an actor might wear in a community theater performance. The only parts of the getup that look convincing are the two guns. She knows the Taser is the real thing, and the pistol looks authentic as well. Its weight makes the holster sag in the way a prop probably wouldn't.

But besides the weapons, the outfit seems like it would only fool someone on first glance.

Which, she realizes, is exactly what happened. She and Leo only glanced at the guy when he first entered the house. They never had a chance to really study his appearance.

The agent continues to badger Leo, but Sue isn't paying attention to the words. She continues to scrutinize the man. He has a tall, stocky body. From his build, he looks like someone who might have been an athlete when he was younger, but he's since packed on a little too much weight around his midsection.

His fingernails are long, with dirt caked underneath, like a little boy who's been playing in a sandbox all day.

The more she looks, the more she can't believe an SEC agent would go out in public looking this way.

She directs her eyes back to the jacket lying on the chair. The man's badge has fallen out of the jacket pocket and is lying on the floor next to the discarded fedora. She squints. Then her skin goes cold. The badge appears to be a photocopy glued to a piece of cardboard. And it's peeling off.

The man's badge is fake.

He's not who he says he is.

CHAPTER 9

SUE SNAPS OUT OF her thoughts. The man is practically shouting at Leo.

"I don't want to hear any more of these lies," the man says. "Stop covering for the firm."

"I'm not covering up anything," Leo says, keeping his voice as calm as possible. "I'm not lying. I'm not equivocating. I'm being truthful. I'm a sworn officer of the court."

The man laughs and barks, "That's rich."

He pushes two fingers into Leo's chest. Leo squirms away and the man does it again.

"Stop," Sue says. "You're hurting him."

Sue has been so focused on the man that she hasn't been paying attention to Leo. Now she takes a good look at him.

He looks awful.

His skin is pallid and clammy. She can see beads of sweat on his forehead and bald scalp. And his breathing seems to be labored. That wasn't calmness she heard in his voice earlier. He was having trouble speaking.

He looks like he's about to pass out.

Or have a heart attack.

But the man doesn't care, obviously. He keeps pressing his fingers into Leo's chest, barking questions at him.

"Leave him alone," Sue shouts.

She almost adds, *You'll give him a heart attack!* But she doesn't want to put the words out there. If she does, she might stress Leo out even more, push him over the edge.

"I'll leave him alone when he starts telling the truth," the man growls, his teeth clenched.

Sue opens her mouth to protest again, but she hesitates when she hears the ringing of a cell phone.

The man steps back, fumbling in his pocket for his phone.

"Don't you two move," the man orders, as he retreats into the hallway to answer his phone.

"Yeah!" the man says into the phone.

After a moment, he says, "Not yet...He doesn't...I will."

"Leo," Sue whispers. "Are you all right?"

Her husband nods, but he doesn't look all right. His skin is ghost white, and he's doing his best to take long slow breaths.

"Leo," Sue says, glancing up to make sure the man is occupied on the phone. "He isn't from the SEC."

"I know," Leo says, looking at her.

She sees real fear in his eyes.

"His badge is fake," she whispers.

Leo nods. He hadn't noticed this, but he's known for a

long time that the man is pretending to be someone he isn't.

"Nothing about this follows due process," Leo says, holding up his zip-tied wrists. "He's broken a half-dozen laws since he rang our doorbell."

"Oh, Pie," she says, unable to hide the fear in her voice. "What are we going to do?"

"I don't know," Leo says.

They look into the hallway, where the man posing as an SEC agent is pacing back and forth, holding the phone to his ear. He looks nervous, frustrated—frightening.

"We need to call the police," Sue whispers.

Leo's eyes say all he needs to say: *If we try to make a phone call and get caught, there's no telling what the guy will do with us.*

"What about the panic button?" Sue whispers, making sure to keep her voice down.

When their security system was installed, the company put in a panel in Leo's office that allows them to simply press a button to trigger their alarm. The authorities will be called automatically, and a loud siren will begin to wail within the walls of the house.

The only problem, Sue realizes, is that as soon as one of them hits the alarm, the man will know the police are on their way. He has demonstrated that he's unstable and unpredictable. Would he flee right away? Or would he try something crazy before escaping?

Hurt Leo?

Take Sue hostage?

Kill them both?

"I'm going to try a new approach," Leo whispers to Sue. "I'm going to—"

The man storms back into the room.

"I just talked to the boss," the man says, holding up his cell phone for them to see. "She's not happy with what she's hearing. I better get some goddamn answers, and I better get them right now."

CHAPTER 10

"LOOK," LEO SAYS TO the man, taking a tone that suggests cooperation and complicity. "It's getting late. I'm sure we'd all like to get on with our evenings. Please just tell me what you want...what I need to do to make this go away."

Those words—*what I need to do to make this go away*—seem to calm the man. He looks pleased that Leo is willing to play ball.

"Fine," the man says, "I need you to let me into your company files. The private server."

Leo opens his mouth to object—his natural reaction to such an unlawful violation of his privacy—but Sue gives him a pleading look.

"Okay," Leo says. "The computer's across the hall."

"Well, what the hell are you waiting for?" the man says. "Get off your asses and let's go."

Leo and Sue hobble on their zip-tied legs. The man makes hurry-up motions with his hands, but neither Leo nor Sue can move quickly.

In the hallway, the man's attention seems to be focused on Leo. Sue takes this opportunity to try to wriggle free of her wrist restraints. No luck. The plastic is locked around her wrists so tightly that her hands are beginning to turn white.

Inside the office, Sue eyes the telephone on the desk.

And on the wall behind the desk is the panic button.

But the man shoves them over toward the love seat at the other end of the room. Leo offers to help, but the man dismisses the offer and orders him to tell him his password.

"Twist and Shout," Leo says. "All one word. Capital T. Capital S. Those are our cats," he adds, trying to sound friendly.

Inside, Leo feels ill. The man will be able to access the firm's client list and inner-office communication, which the partners like to keep secret.

The man settles into the seat of Leo's leather wingback office chair, again easing himself down as if the act of sitting hurts. The man's shirt has come untucked, and as he leans against the back rest, Sue can spot a glimpse of the man's skin on his lower back.

No—not his skin.

A beige-colored fabric appears to be fastened to his lower back. It looks like a pain patch—the kind that secretes pain-relieving medicine into the skin.

Who is this guy? Sue wonders.

The man rolls up his sleeves—there's another pain patch on his arm. His hands fly over the keyboard and move the mouse around with lightning speed. Even watching him from across the room, Sue and Leo can tell that the man is very comfortable with computers. Since he walked into their home, the man has seemed out of place. He looks like a thug, dresses strangely, and acts unstable. But now, in front of a computer, he looks at home for the first time.

He obviously has experience with computers—and with the kind of data that Leo's files hold. The company uses complicated spreadsheets and legal documents, neither of which can be easily navigated without knowledge of the legal profession and high technological literacy.

The man seems to have both.

For the first time, he actually seems to have skills that Sue and Leo might expect of an SEC agent.

But Sue reminds herself of the weird cardboard badge and all the other unprofessional warning signs, starting with the man blasting Leo with a Taser as soon as he walked in the door.

There is no way this man could be from the SEC, Sue thinks. *But then who is he?*

Meanwhile, Leo is studying the man as well. He still can't place where he's seen him before. There is something familiar about his face . . .

"Why don't you let me help you find what you're looking for so we can all call it a night?" Leo says, trying to sound as sincere as possible.

"Don't play all innocent, Leo. You know what you did. You can act all fatherly and supportive, but really, you're not a very good person."

As he says this, the man's right eyebrow raises slightly, which triggers a flash of a memory for Leo.

CHAPTER 11

LEO IS SITTING IN his office, typing a memo on his computer, when a shadow passes by the glass window on his door. He looks up, but whoever it was has already passed by.

He looks back at the file when he hears footsteps in the hall. Someone—a big man by the sound of it—is heading back in the direction of Leo's office.

This time, the person stops at the office door and faces the glass.

The glass is textured, like the door of a shower, and it obscures what is on the other side. But Leo can make out a man's silhouette, big and broad, taking up most of the glass panel.

Whoever it is, he is looking into Leo's office. He steps forward and puts his face right up to the glass, making his features more distinguishable. Leo can see a mouth, a nose, eyes—all blurry and unrecognizable—on a distorted peach-colored face.

Leo is sure the man can't see him any better than Leo can see him. Leo figures he probably appears as little more than an unrecognizable human-shaped blob behind the desk.

But the man's face changes, as if he likes what he sees. His mouth curves into a big blurry grin. And Leo can see well enough to notice one eyebrow raise involuntarily, as if pulled up by a fishhook.

Even through the blurry glass, the expression is disquieting. This isn't the friendly smile of an old friend dropping by unannounced. Or a fellow lawyer coming to ask Leo to lunch.

The smile reminds Leo of something he recently saw on a Discovery Channel documentary: a hyena grinning maniacally when it spotted its prey.

Leo opens his mouth to call out to the stranger, but the man quickly turns away and disappears from view.

Leo rises to his feet and steps warily across his office carpet. He cracks his door and peeks out, seeing a man tromping down the hallway in work boots, jeans, and a baggy hooded sweatshirt.

Leo steps into the hallway and calls out, "Can I help you, sir?"

The man keeps walking but turns his head slightly, just enough to give Leo a glimpse of his profile. There is that one eyebrow raised again.

The man lifts his hand in a goodbye gesture, and then he disappears into the stairwell. Leo stares at the door. His pulse is racing, and he's not sure why. He tells himself not to be bothered by the encounter.

He's sure he'll never see the man—whoever he is—again.

CHAPTER 12

LEO AND SUE SIT quietly as the man searches on the computer. The only sounds are the chatter of the man's fingers over the keypad and a clock that hangs on the wall, clicking away the seconds.

Leo doesn't know what to do. His undershirt beneath his sweater is wet with his sweat, and he feels alternating waves of nausea and panic. His heart is thudding in his chest, and he doesn't know how much more of this stress he can take.

Sue seems to be keeping it together better, Leo thinks. She has always been strong, able to carry a heavy burden. Leo internalizes his stress, which was part of the problem with his heart. But Sue is more of a doer, a fighter. He knows it's killing her to sit with her mouth closed and not tell this crazy son of a bitch to get the hell out of their house.

But Leo thinks antagonizing the man will only make matters worse. He wants to wait out this bizarre "interrogation"—or whatever you'd call it—without incensing their captor. The so-called agent seems volatile, and the only way to get out of this, Leo thinks, is to keep from throwing any gasoline on the fire already burning inside him.

It's been Leo's experience, after more than thirty years in courtrooms, that cooler heads usually prevail.

Suddenly, the man slams the palm of his hand down on the desk and snaps, "Oh, for Christ's sake!"

Both Leo and Sue jerk, startled by the outburst.

"What are you trying to hide, Leo?" the man snarls.

"Hide?"

"This," the man says, gesturing to the computer screen even though Leo can't read it from across the room. "This file marked 'admin' is empty. When did you purge those files?"

Leo shakes his head in bafflement. He vaguely remembers creating a folder for administrative notes, but he never put anything in it.

"If you would just tell me what you're looking for," Leo says, "maybe I could help you."

"Yeah, right," the man says, turning back to the computer. "That way, you could steer me in the wrong direction. I'm not giving you an opportunity to obfuscate this process any more than you already have. I know what I'm d—"

A beeping noise resounds from down the hall, and the man jumps out of his seat.

"What is that?" he shouts, his hand going for the pistol in his shoulder holster. "An alarm? Did you—"

"It's the oven timer." Sue practically shouts to make sure the man doesn't draw his gun and start waving it around.

The man looks at her and listens with an expression on his face of utter confusion, as if he's never heard an oven timer in his entire life.

"Oh," the man says, apparently finally convinced that the noise he hears isn't an alarm.

He settles back into the chair and goes back to work on the computer.

The timer continues to beep.

"Would you like me to go turn it off?" Sue asks.

"No."

Beep...Beep...Beep.

She waits, nonplussed, for almost a full minute.

"If I don't get the chicken out of the oven, it's going to burn," Sue says.

Without looking up from the computer screen, the man flicks his wrist at her as if to say, *I don't care if it burns. Stop talking.*

Sue considers saying nothing, but judging by the man's reaction to the oven timer going off, she would hate to see what this guy will do if the actual fire alarm goes off.

Beep...Beep...Beep.

"Sir," Sue says, her voice like a teacher talking to an elementary school student. "If someone doesn't take the chicken out of the oven, then there's going to be a whole lot of smoke in the kitchen. And if that happens, another alarm—a real alarm—will go off."

This statement—no doubt using the word "alarm"—wakes the man up.

"Now would you like me to go take the chicken out of the oven?" Sue says, rising to her feet. "Just cut these ties around my legs and I'll do it in a jiffy."

"Sit down," the man orders. "I'll do it."

He rises to his feet and heads toward the door. He mutters, disgusted, "Jesus . . . you people."

As soon as he's gone, Sue rises to her feet. Her legs tremble.

"Muffy," Leo hisses, "what are you doing?"

Sue points to the alarm panel on the wall across the room.

"It's worth a try," she says.

"Wait," Leo hisses. "You saw how he reacted from the oven timer. What do you think he'll do to us if the alarm starts blaring through the house?"

Sue hesitates.

The clock on the wall ticks loudly, counting the seconds until the man returns.

CHAPTER 13

BEEP...BEEP...BEEP.

The man with the gun walks down the hall and into the living room. He can't believe this house. It must be worth a million dollars. It's spacious, even though there are certainly larger mansions in the city, but what really strikes him is the décor. Everything in the house tells him that Leo Fisher has money to burn. There is a huge L-shaped couch and a large, comfortable-looking recliner, both upholstered in leather. The walls are decorated with expensive-looking landscape paintings. Hardwood flooring stretches from wall to wall, with a plush rug in the center of the room.

Not only does the big room with expensive-looking accoutrements impress him, but the house is clean from floor to ceiling. There isn't a dust bunny on the carpet or cobweb on the ceiling. A bookshelf along the wall looks like it's dusted every day.

Obviously, Leo Fisher has enough money for a maid to come and clean multiple times a week.

Some people really do have it all, the man thinks. *There's no way someone gets this rich by being honest.*

The man has no doubt Leo Fisher is an unscrupulous lawyer.

Devious. Deceitful. Corrupt.

As crooked as a bolt of lightning.

The man knows it—he just needs to find the evidence.

He follows the beeping sound past a dining room with a crystal chandelier over the table to a big kitchen with marble countertops and polished terra-cotta floors.

Tendrils of smoke creep from the oven door. A cloud hovers just under the ceiling.

"Oh, for Christ's sake," the man says, flinging open the oven door.

A heat wave hits his face, and a fresh cloud of smoke billows out.

"Damn it!"

He's afraid the smoke detector will go off any minute. He looks around the kitchen, trying to find oven mitts so he can take out the casserole dish. He flings open drawers and cabinet doors. Finally, he finds a pile of dish towels. He takes two towels and grabs the casserole dish and flings it into the sink with a clatter.

The oven is still beeping madly.

Beep…Beep…Beep.

He looks around for a smoke detector in this room and sees none. He ventures to the living room, where one is mounted above the doorway. The air in here is hazy with smoke.

He starts waving the towel in front of the detector. He has to stretch to even get close to the detector, and, as he does so, he feels a sharp ripping pain in his lower back.

He grunts in agony and doubles over, holding one hand on his knee with the other twisted around, holding his back.

He grits his teeth.

"I swear to Christ," he growls, "if that goddamn fire alarm goes off, I'm going to kill both of them and be done with it."

CHAPTER 14

SUE HEARS THE CLATTER of the casserole pan in the sink.

She's tired of arguing with Leo. She has to do something. She turns away from her husband and begins shuffling across the room. Her leg restraints keep her from moving fast, but all she has to do is get close enough to the panic button to lunge for it.

She expects Leo to whisper for her to stop, but he is silent. Maybe he's finally given in and realizes she's right.

The timer on the oven is still bleeping from down the hall.

Beep . . . Beep . . . Beep.

Sue assumes she's safe as long as the beeping noise is audible. She knows that's a risky assumption—the man could be headed back right now, without bothering to turn it off—but it's a risk she's willing to take.

Halfway across the room, she pauses for a glance over her shoulder. She freezes when she sees Leo.

He isn't being quiet because he agrees with her course of action. He's quiet because he can't breathe! He's gone as pale as a sheet, and he's pulling at the collar of his shirt. His chest heaves, and a wheezing sound escapes from his throat.

"Oh, Pie," Sue says, and she freezes.

What should she do? she thinks.

Help Leo?

Or go for the alarm?

CHAPTER 15

THE MAN WAVES THE towel in front of the fire alarm a few more times and is finally satisfied that there isn't enough smoke to set it off.

He heads back toward the office.

Beep...Beep...Beep.

He stops—the goddamn timer is still going off.

"Son of a bitch," he snaps, stomping back to the kitchen.

The room is still filled with smoke. He's just lucky there isn't a smoke alarm in here.

He looks over the buttons, trying to figure out what to press in order to shut the goddamn stove up. He presses something, and the oven turns off, but not the timer. Gritting his teeth in frustration, he starts pounding buttons.

Beep...Beep...Be—

Suddenly, the house is silent. But not completely silent. He can hear whispering coming from the office where he left Sue and Leo.

Furious, the man storms back through the house.

He puts his hand on the gun in his shoulder holster.

CHAPTER 16

SUE MAKES HER DECISION. She turns back to help Leo.

Almost as soon as she starts his way, his breathing seems to relax a little. He was just so scared that she was making the wrong decision that he worked himself into a frenzy.

"Are you okay?" she whispers as she arrives at his side.

He nods. Instead of talking, he concentrates on taking long, deep breaths. He inhales through his nose, exhales through his mouth.

He looks terrible. The last time she saw his skin look this pallid was when he had his heart attack.

Oh, God, she thinks. *I don't know what to do.*

She looks back over her shoulder at the panic button across the room. Is there still time? Suddenly, she notices something.

Silence.

The beeping noise has stopped. How long has it been

since he turned it off? The answer comes with the sound of the man's footsteps stomping through the house, getting closer. Just by the clomping of his feet, Sue can tell the guy is mad.

A wave of nausea runs through her body. She feels like she could throw up.

This gives her an idea.

"Just relax," she whispers to Leo. "I'm going to try something else."

"What are you going to do?" Leo wheezes.

"Pie." She grabs his hands and clutches them to her chest. "You've got to trust me."

CHAPTER 17

"WHAT THE HELL IS going on in here?" the man barks as he enters the room.

Sue is on her hands and knees on the carpet.

"I'm going to throw up," Sue says, contorting her body in a retching motion.

She is acting, but only a little. She does in fact feel ill, so she only has to exaggerate. If she had to go so far as actually vomit, she could probably do it.

"Please," Leo says in a hoarse voice, "you have to help my wife."

Thank you for going along with my plan, Leo, Sue thinks.

She had been worried he wouldn't.

The man stands over her. She can feel his irritation radiating from his skin.

"Oh, for Christ's sake," he says in a huff, like a parent exasperated with an uncooperative child. "Come on," the man growls, grabbing her by the arm and yanking her to her feet. "Where's the bathroom?"

She points across the hall to their bedroom, where the

interrogation began. He drags her toward the door. Her ankles are still in restraints, so she has to hobble. The man is impatient, pulling her along. At the doorway, she loses her balance but catches herself on the wall. Finally, they get to the bathroom door. Before shoving her inside, the man looks around in the room, as if to make sure there aren't any weapons or a big window she can climb out of.

"If you need to puke," he orders, "then go ahead. Or splash some water on your face. Whatever. Just get your shit together, woman."

He slams the door, leaving Sue inside.

Now what do I do? she thinks.

She pretends to make dry-heaving sounds as she looks around the room frantically. She uses the gagging noises to cover the sound of her opening drawers and the doors underneath the sink. She finds a small pair of fingernail clippers. A plunger. The pink razor she uses to shave her legs. A nail file.

If she was James Bond she might be able to use one of these as a weapon, but there's nothing here that would help her stand up to this guy, with his stun gun and what she is sure is a very real handgun.

She considers the lid on the back of the toilet. It's certainly heavy enough it could knock a man unconscious, but it's not something she could wield easily. It's not as if she could hide it behind her back as she came out of the bathroom. She realizes there is nothing in here that she could use as a weapon.

She flushes the toilet and then stands by the door to listen.

She has another idea.

CHAPTER 18

SUE IS THINKING OF the phone in the bedroom. If the man is preoccupied with Leo, she might be able to sneak out and make a quick, quiet call to 911.

All she needs to do is dial the number, whisper that they have an intruder, and tell them the address. Or maybe she doesn't even need to do that—maybe they can trace the call.

Either way, a phone call will alert the authorities without sounding a loud alarm inside the house that might send the man over the edge.

Sue listens at the door. She hears the man shuffling back and forth in the hallway, muttering.

He's on the phone again.

This means he is preoccupied. The only problem is he is pacing in front of the bedroom door. She can't leave the bathroom without him seeing her.

"Uh huh," he says into the phone. "Yeah."

His voice fades. She thinks she hears his footsteps farther away in the house.

Is this my chance?

She eases open the bathroom door and peeks out. There is no sign of the man. She takes a step into the bedroom, but then something catches her eyes. Outside the window in their bedroom, a light is going off and on.

Sue takes a moment to hop to the window and look out. The bedroom window faces the front of the house, and she can tell that someone—the man, presumably—is flicking the front porch light off and on.

The unfamiliar SUV is still parked on the side of the road, and Sue sees the light come on inside as someone opens the door. A person—a woman—steps out of the car and walks up the driveway, briskly but coolly.

Whoever she is, she has an air of confidence about her.

This must be the man's accomplice, the person he's been talking to on the phone. Sue wants to hear what they have to say to each other, but she's wasting precious time.

She has a phone call to make.

She takes two shuffling steps toward the nightstand and the phone on top of it. Then she freezes. She hears something coming from the office—a low, agonizing moan. Then the sound of a loud thump resounds through the corridor.

Sue can tell what the sound is—Leo has just collapsed onto the floor.

"Pie," she calls, her voice thick with panic.

She shuffles as fast as she can across the hall to her husband, forgetting about the telephone that was only a few steps from her reach.

CHAPTER 19

LEO IS LYING ON his side on the carpet, wincing in pain and clutching his chest.

"Oh, my God, Leo!"

Sue collapses to his side.

"Breathe, Pie, breathe."

The man's footsteps clamor down the hallway. He bursts into the room like a bull let out of the chute.

"What the hell's going on in here?" he growls.

"You have to call an ambulance," Sue says. "Leo could be having a heart attack."

The man freezes for a moment, studying Leo and Sue. He smirks.

"He's not having a heart attack," the man says. "He'll be fine."

The man leans over and grabs Leo's arm.

"Sit up," he orders, and between the man and Sue, they get him to sit upright, leaning against the foot of the love seat.

"Is it a heart attack, Leo?" Sue says. "Is your left arm numb? Do you feel shooting pains?"

Leo looks clammy and sick—on the verge of puking or passing out—but Sue can see that he is not having a heart attack. Not yet. He is having chest pains. No doubt about it. But they haven't reached the level of cardiac arrest.

"Please," she pleads to the man. "This has to stop. He can't take much more of this."

"Leo," the man says, snapping his fingers to get his attention. "I need you to hang in there. This is almost over."

His demeanor is different. The anger has subsided for a moment.

"There's been a change of plans," the man says. "I just talked to my boss. She's not happy with how things are going. She wants me to question Leo alone. She thinks maybe he's holding something back because you're here, Susan."

Sue stares at him in disbelief.

"Maybe he doesn't want you to know about all the shady business he's been up to," the man says.

"That's ridiculous," Sue says, but her mind is racing.

Could it be true? She knows this psychopath is not with the SEC, as he claimed, but for the life of her, she cannot figure out who he is or why he might be here. Is the firm caught up in something illegal?

She doesn't believe Leo would willingly do anything unscrupulous, but maybe his hands are tied.

Sue is still trying to figure out what she thinks about all this when the man grabs her by her arm and tugs her to her feet.

"Here's what's going to happen," the man says, his voice now calm and, for the first time tonight, sounding almost professional. "You're going to go back into the bathroom for fifteen minutes. Leo and I are going to have a little chat, just the two of us. And then I'll get out of your hair and this will all be over. Capiche?"

As he's talking, the man is pulling her toward the door. She looks back at Leo, who is leaning against the couch. They lock eyes, and she can see the terror in his expression.

She has never seen someone so frightened.

"It's almost over, Pie," she says, trying to sound as reassuring as she can. She hopes he can hold on for fifteen minutes. "Just try to stay calm. Remember: deep breaths."

The man pulls her into the hallway, and she feels the overwhelming need to cry. She has the same feeling she did when paramedics wheeled Leo into the ambulance after his heart attack.

She feels with terrifying certainty that she will never see her husband again.

CHAPTER 20

THE MAN DRAGS SUE toward the bathroom door and then shoves her into the room. He pushes her harder than he needs to, and she has to catch herself with the counter to avoid falling.

"Fifteen minutes," she says. "Then I'm coming out."

She tries to come across as strong, but the words sound more like questions than statements. She is using all of her willpower not to cry.

The man nods, as if bored by her.

Sue checks her watch.

It's 9:04.

The man says, "If Leo does what I want, and you stay in the bathroom, this will all be over soon. If not..." He gives Sue a sinister grin. "Who knows?"

Sue's skin goes cold. Her mind reels, thinking of the possibilities. What exactly is the threat he's making?

Does he mean he'll kill Leo?

Kill both of them?

Rape her?

The way his beady eyes are staring at her, she isn't sure what his intentions are.

She can't believe she's living through this nightmare. She feels as if her whole world has been turned upside down. She's lived sixty-one years only to find out that the world she thought she understood doesn't exist.

She knew that the world wasn't always fair, but she didn't know that it was crazy. One minute you could be cooking dinner for your husband. The next—a madman forces his way into your house.

"Don't hurt Leo," Sue says to the man. Her chin quivers. "He's a good man."

"Ha," the man huffs. "He's got you fooled just like every-one else."

With that, he slams the door so hard the walls shake. Sue flinches from the sound and jerks away.

"Don't hurt him!" she shrieks and pounds on the door with her fist.

The sound of her voice reverberates within the small bathroom, and the terror she hears in her own voice frightens her even more.

She catches sight of herself in the mirror and does a double-take. She hardly recognizes the woman reflected back at her. Behind the lenses of her glasses, her eyes are red and puffy from crying. Her hair is a tangled, sweaty mess.

No use feeling sorry for herself. She has to remain strong.

She puts her head against the door and listens. She can hear muffled voices, the loud bombast of the man and the softer, pained sound of her husband.

The phone in their bedroom is only about ten feet away. Should she risk going for it? Or should she wait the fifteen minutes to see if the man really does leave?

She knows what Leo would want her to do.

Wait.

He wouldn't want to risk antagonizing the man. *Play along*, Leo would say. *Don't do anything to push him over the edge.*

Okay, Sue thinks. *I'll wait.*

But I'm not going to sit here idly.

She pulls open the drawer next to the sink and finds the nail file she spotted earlier. She sits down on the toilet, leans over, and begins sawing at the zip tie on her ankles.

When fifteen minutes is up, she thinks, *I'm coming out and calling the police.*

Or I'm going to die trying.

CHAPTER 21

LEO HEARS THE FOOTSTEPS of the man coming back to the office. Leo feels a minor relief, knowing that Sue is in the bathroom, away from the man.

He hates to see Sue suffering because of him.

"Okay, Leo," the man says, standing over Leo. "Last chance to confess. Is there anything you want to tell me without the wife around? Something you know you did wrong?"

Leo is sitting on the carpet, slumped against the love seat. He feels incredibly weak. He wants to fall over, put his face into the thick carpet, and close his eyes.

The man kneels down next to Leo.

"Did you hear me, old man?" the man snaps.

"I have no secrets from Sue," Leo says slowly, making a great effort to speak. "I really don't know what you're—"

The man's hand lashes out like a whip and smacks Leo hard across the face. Pain shoots through his jaw and cheekbone.

The man grabs Leo by the collar and holds Leo's face inches from his.

"Listen here, you lying little parasite," the man snarls through gritted teeth. "If you don't tell me what I want to know, you're going to feel more pain than you've ever felt in your life."

Leo is speechless, terrified—his heart pounding a hundred miles a minute—as he stares into the face of his assailant.

The man growls, "Your heart attack will seem like a vacation compared to what I'm going to do to you."

CHAPTER 22

THE BLADE OF THE nail file breaks through the plastic strip, and suddenly Sue's legs are free.

She checks her watch.

It's 9:12.

"It's been more than ten minutes," Sue yells through the bathroom door. "Can I come out now?"

"No," shouts the man. "We agreed on fifteen minutes. Stay in there."

She checks her watch again, unable to view the hands of the clock because of her trembling arms. She clutches her hands together to try to stop her wrists from shaking. The second hand on her watch seems to be moving at a glacial pace.

She places the blade of the nail file over the plastic strip binding her wrists. It's harder than it was with her ankles because she can't get a good grip on the file. She has it squeezed between her fingers and can't seem to saw against the plastic with any strength.

"Come on," she whispers.

A rivulet of sweat crawls from her hairline and rolls down the side of her face.

She tries to listen, but she just can't make out what Leo and the man are saying. The man's voice is the most distinguishable, but it sounds like a series of grunts and growls instead of actual words.

She can't really hear anything from Pie.

He might be talking, she thinks, but with his heart about to explode, he's probably not speaking much above a whisper.

She thinks she hears a smacking sound. She heard it earlier and thought perhaps it was the man clapping his hands together as he paced in front of Leo.

But this time the smacking noise is followed by the unmistakable sound of Leo crying out in pain.

"Please stop," Leo begs, his voice louder now, and audible.

"Pie," Sue screams. "Are you okay?"

Silence is her only response. She redoubles her sawing efforts with the nail file.

Almost there.

CHAPTER 23

"SHUT THE HELL UP in there!" the man roars at Sue.

He stands over Leo, who has slid down and is now lying in a fetal position, curled up on the carpet. His cheeks are bright with red marks in the shape of handprints. A small trickle of blood is leaking from a busted lip.

"You're not going to tell me what I need to know, are you, Leo?"

Leo says nothing. He is nearly catatonic. He is trying to concentrate only on his breathing. His mouth has never felt so dry in all his life.

"Okay," the man says, kneeling next to Leo. "If I can't get information from you, you're going to pay in another way. Where's your safe? Where do you keep your money?"

Leo turns his head, waking up a bit from his stupor. Maybe this is almost over. All of this has been the charade for a simple robbery. He just needs to tell the invader where the money is, and then maybe he'll finally leave.

"There's a couple hundred dollars in my wallet," Leo says. "It's in the kitch—"

"I'm not talking about a couple hundred dollars," the man snaps. "I'm talking about your stacks of cash. Where do you keep them?"

"Stacks of cash?" Leo says.

"Yeah," the man says, flustered. "In your safe. You've got at least a hundred grand here, don't you?"

"We don't have a safe," Leo says. "I don't keep much cash in the house."

"Are you joking with me? Do you think I'm stupid? You're a millionaire. What about gold? How many gold bricks do you have?"

Leo shakes his head.

"If you want," Leo says, "we can go to an ATM and I'll make a withdrawal. I think I can withdraw five hundred dollars in a single day. Or maybe it's only three hundred. I'm not sure."

"You goddamn rich people," the man says, disgusted. He stands up and begins pacing. "You ruin people's lives and don't have a care in the goddamn world. You don't give a damn about who you hurt just to make yourself richer and richer. And you put your money in the goddamn bank and just let it sit there. Other people could really use that money, you selfish, greedy bastard."

As the man paces, his voice gets louder and louder. His face turns red. Blood vessels stand out on his forehead. Spit flies from his lips as he talks—more to himself than to Leo.

His anger is building to a new level of ferocity.

"You think you can get away with anything," he growls. "Well, not today. Today is a day of reckoning for you, Leo. Today, you're finally going to get what's coming to you."

"This isn't right," Leo croaks. "I didn't do anything."

"You rotten, sniveling excuse for a human being. You made promises and you lied. *You lied!*"

Leo asks, in earnest, "Promises to whom?"

The man is taken aback.

"You don't even know what did, do you? You destroyed her . . . after all she did for you. You're gonna pay!"

CHAPTER 24

THE BLADE OF THE nail file slices through the last millimeter of plastic. Sue can hardly believe it—her hands and free of their restraints.

Sue can tell the conversation—if you could call it that—is becoming more and more heated. She can hear the terror in Leo's voice and the anger in the man's.

She checks her watch.

It's been fifteen minutes.

She takes a deep breath.

Okay, she tells herself. *It's time to act.*

Sue clutches the door handle with trembling fingers and swings it open quietly. For a moment, Leo and the man are silent. Sue steps out onto the carpet.

She looks at the phone on her side of the bed, then lets her eyes scan toward the door. She takes a few gingerly steps forward, keeping her eyes fixed on the doorway. In another step or two, she should be able to see across the hall to where Leo and the man are located.

Now she hears noises—some kind of scuffle.

Grunting.

She takes another step forward, and all of the muscles in her body lock up in terror.

The man is holding Leo down with a pillow over his face. In his other arm, the man is holding a knife. He drives the blade down, stabbing it into Leo's neck.

Leo squirms.

His face is free for a moment, and he screams, "Muffy, he's killing me!"

The man laughs—a jovial sort of chuckle that sounds all the more sadistic because it doesn't match what's happening. The laugh sounds like it's coming from someone watching a sitcom on TV, not a murderer in the act of killing someone.

Sue's paralysis breaks. She opens her mouth and screams as loud as she can, *"Noooo!"*

She rushes forward. In a flash, the man drops the knife, reaches for his holster, and spins around with the gun aimed at Sue's face. Sue stops short at the bedroom's threshold.

She has time only to draw in a quick, terrified breath before the man shoots her in the head.

CHAPTER 25

LEO SEES THE MUZZLE flash out of the corner of his eye and hears the thunderous bark of the pistol. But his attention is on Sue. A tuft of her hair blows out from her head, as if she's been hit by a puff of air.

His wife of forty-one years staggers backward and falls onto the carpet.

Leo tries to sit upright, craning is his neck to see Sue, flailing with one arm and holding his bleeding neck with the other. Blood coats his hand and is dripping onto the carpet. The man, who is still crouched over him, is also splattered in blood.

Stars burst in Leo's vision—and he fears that at any moment he's going to pass out.

And then I won't wake up, he thinks.

He isn't sure this is a bad thing. If Muffy is dead, then he can't imagine going on living without her.

But then a miracle happens.

His wife sits up.

Blood is dripping from her hairline down the side of her face. She reaches up and tentatively touches a spot on the side of her head where her hair is matted and dark red.

Sue looks confused—unsure how she's still alive.

Her eyes are alert. Her face is full of determination. Leo's heart swells with relief.

That's my Muffy, he thinks. *Nothing can stop her.*

Then horror overtakes him as the man rises to his feet. He holsters his gun and bends down to pick up his knife.

Leo wants to stand up, wants to fight the man off. He digs down, tries to find the strength. He's never wanted anything this badly in his life. He *has* to stop this man!

He rolls onto his stomach and crawls, watching the man walk toward Sue.

Leo makes it as far as the hallway. But the room is getting darker, as if someone is dimming the lights. And Leo can't find the strength he desperately needs. His heart—beating so painfully hard earlier—seems to be slowing down. Leo's whole body feels numb.

All he can do is lie on the floor and watch.

Sue rises to her feet and flops onto the bed, crawling toward the telephone on the other side. The man grabs her by the sweater and pins her against the mattress.

The man raises his knife and brings it down—again and again—into her back, shoulders, and neck.

Sue's body goes limp.

CHAPTER 26

WHEN HE FEELS HER body go lifeless beneath him, the man climbs off Sue and stands at the edge of the bed, watching her. His chest is heaving and his back muscles are screaming in pain.

That took a lot out of him.

But it looks like he finally got the job done. Sue is lying facedown, with blood spots growing all over her white sweater, crimson flowers blooming in the snow. Her face is obscured by strands of her hair, a fistful of which is sticky with what looks like strawberry jam.

Her glasses are lying on the comforter, the lenses spattered with blood.

"Crazy bitch," the man mutters.

He reaches out and pokes Sue's buttocks with the knife blade to make sure she's dead. Satisfied, he pockets his knife and moves to wipe sweat off his forehead with his shirtsleeve, but he notices blood splatters on the fabric. He looks down at himself. There is blood all over his clothes—both Sue's and Leo's.

He huffs, annoyed, and grabs his coat off the floor, and then his hat. He positions the fedora on his head, taking some pride in the act. He feels like the hero in an old black-and-white noir film.

He walks out into the hall, where Leo is lying on his side, holding his hand to his throat in a mess of congealed blood. His eyes are barely open and he is still breathing, but the man can see that Leo Fisher won't last much longer. His skin is pale, his lips practically purple. Leo looks like a zombie in a low-budget horror movie.

The man laughs. *Leo Fisher is a zombie*, he thinks. *He's dead but just doesn't know it yet.*

The smell of gunpowder lingers, but a strange coppery scent dominates the air, like a perfume added to cover the unpleasant odor of gunfire. That perfume, the man realizes with a grin, must be the smell of blood.

The man steps past Leo and looks around on the carpet for the shell casing from his Cobra .380. When he locates it, he tucks it into his pocket. He looks at the computer and the desk and considers what to do about his fingerprints. He walks back across the hall and sifts through the pile of Leo's clothes on the floor. He grabs a pair of boxer shorts and walks back to the office. He wipes down the keyboard and mouse on the computer. Then moves to the surface of the desk. He whistles while he works. He feels quite jovial.

He was getting more and more angry as he questioned Leo, that lying bastard, but now that the job is over, he feels a certain calm contentment about the whole thing.

It didn't go as well as he'd hoped—he would like to be leaving here with a bag full of money or some valuable information. Or both.

But the main goal has been accomplished—killing Leo Fisher.

The man looks around, trying to remember if he touched anything else. Wiping off his fingerprints is probably unnecessary, he thinks, but there's no harm in being overly cautious.

When he's satisfied he's eliminated any prints he might have left, he walks back over to where Leo is lying on the floor. He drops the boxers on the floor next to the dying man. Then he pulls out his cell phone.

Staring at Leo, the man punches numbers on his phone and waits.

CHAPTER 27

LEO STARES UP FROM the floor at the man who murdered his wife.

The man holds a cell phone to his ear, waiting for the person on the other end to pick up. The man is carrying himself as if this is just another phone call, as if he's at the grocery store and is calling home to see if he needs to pick up more milk.

Leo is close enough to the man to hear the woman's voice on the other end of the line.

"Is it done?" she says, her voice muffled and unrecognizable through the phone.

"Yeah," the man says. "He went down easy."

The female voice says something Leo can't make out, and the man chuckles in response.

"Sometimes it just doesn't work out," the man says, and both he and the woman laugh together.

There's something about the way the man says, "Sometimes it just doesn't work out."

It's as if the man is saying an inside joke—something he and this woman must say to each other, like a quote from a movie that they both find ridiculous. Or something that was once said to one of them that they've since talked about often—so much it's now a punchline to them.

The man is still talking to the woman on the phone, but Leo's thoughts drift elsewhere. His mind is a murky fog— he's barely conscious—but he has the feeling again that he knows this man from somewhere.

The phrase echoes through the cloudy canyons of his mind—*Sometimes it just doesn't work out.*

CHAPTER 28

LEO STANDS AT THE desk of his employee Alecia Schmuhl as she packs up her belongings into a cardboard box. Her eyes are puffy because she's been crying.

Leo hates to see her like this. He never likes terminating people, but firing Alecia is especially painful.

"You're going to make a great lawyer someday," Leo says.

"Just not here," Alecia says spitefully.

She takes a framed photograph—the last of her possessions— and tosses it onto the top of the box.

"Please don't feel bad," Leo says. "Sometimes it just doesn't work out."

Alecia lifts the box, and Leo's eyes drop for an instant to the photograph. It's a picture of Alecia and her husband. Leo knows his name but has never met him, but the sight of the two of them looking happy makes Leo feel even worse, so he looks away. His eyes only drift over the image of her husband for a split second.

He doesn't expect to see Alecia again.

And he certainly doesn't expect to see her husband two weeks later—ringing the doorbell of Leo's home pretending to be an SEC agent.

CHAPTER 29

FOR LEO, THE WORLD seems to darken and then lighten, darken and lighten, as if someone is standing at the light switch, constantly adjusting the dimmer.

He knows what's happening—he's slipping in and out of consciousness.

He rouses awake for a moment and notices the man—the psychopath who invaded his home—is still standing over him, talking on the telephone.

"Cool," the man says to whomever he's talking to. "Meet me at the front door."

With that, the man pockets the phone. He bends over at the waist and puts his hands on his knees. He stares at Leo.

"Guess what, Leo?" the man says cheerfully, like a friend who has good news. "You're going to die."

Then the man's face changes from merry to mad. He clenches his teeth and stands. He pulls one leg back like a soccer player ready to make a penalty kick. When he drives the toe of his shoe into the side of Leo's head, fresh lightning bolts explode through Leo's skull.

Instead of knocking Leo out, the blow has the opposite effect—it wakes him up.

As the man walks away, Leo feels a burst of energy. He sits up, grabs the underwear from the floor, and holds the cloth against his bleeding neck. He crawls on his knees and one hand down the hallway.

He makes it to the end of the hallway, where he can see through the living room to the foyer. The front door is wide open, and a woman is approaching on the walkway, carrying some kind of object. It looks like a milk jug, only bigger.

The man leans down, and the two embrace with a long, tongue-filled kiss.

When they break apart, the man shifts his body, and Leo can see the woman's face better.

Leo squints his eyes.

"Alecia?"

She was behind all of this?

The woman he'd fired from Bean, Kinney & Korman hands the object she's carrying to her husband, Andrew Schmuhl.

"Finish them," Alecia says, and she spins on her heel and heads back down the walkway.

Andrew closes the door and turns around. Leo can make out the object now.

It's a gasoline can.

The thought of being burned alive flashes through Leo's

mind. Then blackness overtakes his vision, and he slumps to the floor.

His last thought before he loses consciousness is that hopefully he'll be dead before Andrew Schmuhl sets him on fire.

CHAPTER 30

SUE DUNCAN OPENS HER EYES.

She rises from the bed to her hands and knees. She fumbles around with her hand and grabs her glasses. Even though they are splattered with blood, she can see better with them.

Through the blood-smeared lenses, she looks around the room and out into the hallway to make sure the intruder isn't near.

She's been playing dead, biding her time.

When the man pulled the trigger of his gun, she'd felt the bullet graze her skull. She'd fallen down, but had realized right away that she was going to live. That's when she'd jumped up and headed for the phone.

But that had been a mistake, because the evil maniac had been on her in seconds. She should have played dead then, she realized.

As the knife came down over and over again, she knew

she couldn't fight him. She had to do what she should have done the second he shot her.

After he jammed the knife into the side of her neck, she closed her eyes, went limp, and held her breath.

It took all her willpower not to scream out in pain and terror. After he left the room, she breathed a slow, silent sigh of relief. But still she didn't get up. The phone was only a few feet away, but she would need time to dial and to speak into the receiver.

So she waited.

As the man talked to Leo. As he talked on the phone. As he whistled as if this was just another day at the office. While he did all these things, Sue waited.

But she hasn't heard him for a while now. From her position on the bed, she can't see either the intruder or Leo. There's a trail of blood in the hallway, but no sign of Leo.

Maybe he's still alive, Sue thinks. *Maybe there's still time to save him.*

She crawls forward. Blood dribbles onto the comforter from the wound in her neck. She grabs the telephone and puts the receiver to her ear and listens for the dial tone.

The line is dead.

The cord is disconnected from the wall. Not just unplugged, she notices—the wire itself is torn. The man must have done that during one of her stays in the bathroom. He must have known what she was thinking.

Sue wants to cry. She wants to give up. This is too much.

But there's still one chance. One last hope.

The panic button.

It's only across the hall, but in her state—with a bullet wound in her head, a deep cut in her neck, and a dozen or more stab wounds on her back and shoulders—it might as well be on the moon.

She has to try.

CHAPTER 31

ANDREW SCHMUHL UNSCREWS THE cap on the can of gasoline and tosses it aside.

He pours a stream of the liquid onto the foyer floor and begins to make a trail through the house. He enters the kitchen and pours some on the stovetop and the kitchen table. He splashes gas on the novel lying on the table. He pours some on the blackened casserole dish in the sink.

He makes his way to the living room where he dumps gasoline all over the big L-shaped couch and the recliner. He douses the lamps and the big rug on the floor.

The air around him quickly smells of chemicals, and Andrew feels euphoric. He can't tell if it's because of the fumes or because he's so happy to be doing what he's doing.

Or both.

Leo is lying on the floor where the living room meets the hallway. Andrew heads that way, planning to douse Leo's body with gasoline, but he was too enthusiastic with his pouring earlier. There's hardly any gas left.

He stands over Leo and flings a few droplets onto his body.

It doesn't matter, Schmuhl thinks. *In about thirty seconds, this whole goddamn house is going to be an inferno.*

He hopes Leo Fisher wakes up long enough to feel the flames blistering his skin.

When Leo takes his final breath, Schmuhl wants him to taste smoke.

CHAPTER 32

SUE LOWERS HERSELF OFF the bed and stands on wobbly legs.

She puts one hand over the gash in her neck, which seems to be bleeding worse than any of her other injuries. Every movement is painful. Her sweater is matted to her back from all the blood, sticking to her skin like she wore it in the shower. Her vision is muddied by the blood on her glasses. And even though she knows what she needs to do, she can't seem to get her legs moving.

Finally, she throws one leg forward. Her muscles contort and strain, doing everything they can to keep her from falling over. She lunges forward with the next step and, again, almost falls over.

She feels like a mummy in an old black-and-white horror movie—unable to move with any speed or grace, only barely able to control her own muscle function.

She gets close to the wall, and she flings her arm out for balance. She leans forward and peeks out the bedroom door.

The crazy intruder is standing near the entrance to the hallway, looming over Leo, who lies unmoving on the ground.

Sue freezes in place. The tremors in her leg muscles expand into earthquakes. She never knew it could be so difficult to do something as simple as stand upright.

Is that gasoline she smells?

My God, she thinks. *What is this maniac going to do? Burn the house down? Hasn't he done enough?*

She wants to give up. Wants to collapse onto the carpet and go to sleep. Leo is already dead, no doubt. What is the point of going on without him?

Out of the corner of her eye, she sees movement. One of their cats—Shout—is standing at the other end of the hallway, near the door to a spare room.

The cat's eyes are wide. The poor thing is terrified.

I have to go on, Sue thinks. *If only to save the cats.*

She peeks around the doorway again. This time, the crazy man has his back turned to her. He is walking away.

Sue takes a deep breath and then hurls herself across the hallway to the office, stumbling like a drunk person. When she gets to the other side, she leans against the wall with her back and then hisses in pain when her stab wounds touch the drywall.

She leans on one shoulder, trying to catch her breath, listening to make sure the psychotic man isn't backtracking to investigate a sound he might have heard.

She eyes the panic button on the other side of the room.

Ten feet away.

To her, it feels like a hundred.

CHAPTER 33

ANDREW SCHMUHL STROLLS THROUGH the foyer and arrives at the front door.

He opens the door to a whoosh of cold November air. A stiff breeze has kicked up while he's been inside.

Andrew sees Alecia waiting for him in the car at the end of the driveway, and looks around to make sure there aren't any other cars or pedestrians.

All is quiet.

Andrew sets the gas can on the concrete walkway and fishes around in his pocket for a book of matches. It's an old book he picked up from a bar a couple weeks ago. There are three matches left.

He plucks one from the book and places it along the sandpaper strip. He scratches the match across the rough surface.

Nothing happens.

He does it again and again, but the strip is worn and he can't get the matchhead to light. Soon the match in his hand is practically shredded, and he discards it in the bushes and grabs another.

CHAPTER 34

SUE SHUFFLES FORWARD, HER breathing heavy, her head pounding, her muscles howling in pain. She's wheezing loudly. Her throat feels like it's constricted to the point where air hardly moves through it. Liquid is running down her face, and she isn't sure if it's sweat or blood.

She makes it to the desk, but the panic button is on the other side. She puts her hands down for support, smearing bloody handprints on the wood.

She hobbles her way around the desk, but the chair is in the way. On any other day, it wouldn't present much of an obstacle. But she can hardly move.

She puts her hands out and pushes the chair in, the wounds in her back screeching as she does it.

A couple more steps.

CHAPTER 35

ANDREW GETS THE SECOND match lit.

"All right," he says, gleeful.

He holds the match out to drop it on the gas puddle just over the threshold. The breeze pushes at his back and the exposed flame blinks out, leaving a wisp of smoke rising from the blackened matchhead.

"Son of a bitch," Andrew mutters.

He tugs the last match out of the book and puts it against the rough lighting strip. If this one doesn't work, it's not a big deal. He'll just have to go into the kitchen and find something else to light the gasoline with. But he's anxious to get out of here.

There are two dead—or near dead—people inside. There's no sense dilly-dallying.

He scrapes the match across the strip and—success!—a flame appears on the first try. Andrew cups his hand around the match. He doesn't want it to go out this time.

He kneels toward the puddle of gasoline with the flame.

CHAPTER 36

SUE TAKES A DEEP breath and lunges for the panic button.

Her palm hits it and pushes it inward. For a moment, nothing happens and Sue feels horror overtake her.

And then sirens start to wail through the walls of the house—a loud, deafening sound that under any other circumstances would make a person instantly throw their hands over their ears.

To Sue Duncan, it's the most beautiful sound she's ever heard.

CHAPTER 37

ANDREW HEARS THE BLEATING alarm and jolts upright.

He looks behind him, expecting to see a police cruiser pulling up to the house. Nothing unusual there. He realizes the sound is coming from the inside.

How can that be?

Andrew turns his head and stares inside. He can see Leo from where he stands. The old man is lying on the floor, just where Andrew left him.

Susan must have done it. Somehow she's still alive.

Well, Andrew thinks, *I'll show you, you crazy bitch.*

He moves to drop the match onto the gasoline. But he stops short, disappointment washing over him in a wave.

The flame has gone out.

He hesitates for a moment, unsure what to do. The siren continues to wail. Panic overtakes him. Andrew grabs the empty gas can and runs down the sidewalk to the getaway car.

CHAPTER 38

SUE'S LEGS GIVE UP their fight, and she plunges to the floor like someone dropping through a trapdoor.

She wants to pass out, but she knows her work isn't done yet. She reaches with her hand and fumbles around on the top of the desk. When her fingers find the telephone, she pulls it down.

She punches 9-1-1.

"Home invasion," she says, mustering all her strength to speak.

She tells the dispatcher the address and explains that she and her husband have been shot and stabbed.

"Please save our cats," she adds, and hangs up the phone.

She gets onto her hands and knees, crawls around the desk, and then blackness overtakes her, pulling her into a deeper sleep than any she's ever known.

Her body collapses facedown on the carpet.

CHAPTER 39

"WHAT THE HELL HAPPENED in there?" Alecia screams at Andrew.

Her foot is pinned to the gas pedal. The tires of the Honda SUV squeal as it flies around a corner. In the backseat, Andrew is trying to remove his bloodstained clothes, but Alecia's driving is throwing him around like a wet sock in a tumble dryer.

"I don't know," he says, tearing open his shirt and sending the buttons flying inside the vehicle.

"Who pulled the alarm, Andrew?" Alecia says. "Who in that house is still alive?"

"It must be Sue," he says. "That crazy bitch is like a cockroach. You can't kill her."

"She's just a little old woman."

"Hell, I shot her in the head," Andrew says, trying to pull his T-shirt off over his head.

"It was a perfect plan, and you messed it up," Alecia says. "Now I'm going to get screwed again."

Alecia takes another curve, and the direction of the car throws Andrew off balance. As he tries to catch himself, his back muscles tighten and he hisses in pain.

"Will you slow down for Christ's sake? We don't want to get pulled over for speeding."

"We need to get the hell out of here."

"Drive like normal," Andrew says. "They don't know who I am. Neither one of them can identify us. Don't worry— we're going to get away with this."

Alecia says nothing but realizes he has a point. She slows the SUV down. She pulls up to a stoplight and tries to act normal. A Honda Odyssey minivan is sitting in the lane next to them, and Alecia risks a sideways glance at its occupants. A man and woman sit in front, chatting. In the back, a DVD player mounted to the ceiling glows for however many kids are sitting back there. These people suspect nothing, which makes Alecia feel some measure of relief.

In the back, Andrew shoves his bloody shirt and jacket into a black garbage bag. He puts the guns in there, both the Taser and the Cobra. He pulls the Velcro tabs on his sneakers and kicks off the shoes, which are also peppered with droplets of blood.

Andrew tells Alecia to give him her telephone, and when she reaches it back to him, he takes out the SIM card inside and breaks it in half. He does the same to his phone and places the pieces into the garbage bag.

"We need to get rid of this stuff," he says. "See if you can find a dumpster somewhere."

He unbuckles his blood-splattered pants and tries to squirm out of them. It's not easy as pain shoots through his lower back.

Alecia drives on, calmer now.

"Tell me this," Alecia says. "Did you at least kill Leo?"

"Yeah," Andrew says. "That son of bitch is dead for sure."

CHAPTER 40

LEO FISHER IS FLOATING.

He must be dead, levitating up out of his body, passing through his living room and into the foyer like a ghost.

There are people walking near him, all of them in uniform. EMTs at his head and feet. A police officer walking next to him. The cop's mouth is moving, but Leo hears no words. All he can hear is strange breathing—is it his?—like Darth Vader from the *Star Wars* movies.

He floats through his front door and down his walkway. He sees flashing lights—red and blue—reflecting off the tree branches overhead.

Leo remembers, all at once, what happened. Andrew Schmuhl zapping him with the Taser, stabbing him with the knife, shooting and stabbing Sue.

Leo realizes what's happening.

He's not floating. He's on a stretcher.

His strange breathing—it's because of an oxygen mask over his mouth.

He becomes aware of something around his neck—medical tape holding a large bandage to his wound.

The paramedics stop the gurney at the back of an ambulance, but before they load him on, the police officer waves for them to wait. As if he's just come up from being underwater, Leo can make out what the officer is saying.

"Wait," the cop says, frantic. "I just need to talk to him for a minute. Leo, can you hear me?"

Leo nods his head as much as he can, which is hardly at all. He reaches up—his arm doesn't feel like it's connected to his own body—and pulls the oxygen mask away.

"Where's Sue?" he asks, his voice hoarse and hardly recognizable.

"She's alive," the officer says, pointing.

Leo turns his head slightly to see paramedics loading another stretcher into a different ambulance. For a moment, Leo doesn't recognize the woman lying prone with an oxygen mask over her face and red paint all over her clothes.

Then he realizes it's Sue.

"Is she going to be okay?" Leo asks, looking around at the paramedics.

They don't tell Leo that the first responding officer had to stick his finger into a gash in Sue's neck to obstruct the blood coming out. Or how shocked the EMTs were by how much blood they found in the house, so much that the first responders think it's a miracle that either of them—let alone both—are still alive.

They don't say any of this, and no one mentions that it

will take another miracle for Sue to make it through the night.

But the looks on their faces say it all—Sue is in bad shape.

"Oh, Muffy," Leo says, and he begins to sob.

"Leo," the officer says, "the EMTs are going to take good care of you and your wife. They're going to do everything they can. But before you go, I need to know—do you know who attacked you?"

Leo's sobs stop, and his face turns to steely resolve.

"Andrew Schmuhl," Leo says.

"Small?"

"Schmuhl," Leo says again, and then he spells the name. "S-C-H-M-U-H-L."

The officer writes the name down.

"He held us hostage for three hours," Leo says. "He tortured us. He tried to kill us both."

"Do you have any idea why?" the officer asks.

"Revenge."

CHAPTER 41

"YOU'RE REALLY FIRING ME?"

Alecia Schmuhl says the words with disbelief in her voice. But Leo isn't sure why she is surprised. This has been a long time coming.

Leo and Sue are sitting in his office in late October. It's a beautiful fall day outside, with golden leaves dancing on tree branches in the bright sunlight.

"It's a decision the partners made," Leo says. "It's not just my decision, but I do agree with it. Your job performance just hasn't been up to par lately."

This is an understatement. In recent weeks, Alecia has missed appointments with clients, failed to file documents by necessary deadlines, come in late, left early, and has done shoddy work in general. And she's been on probation for months after she tried to file paperwork for a home mortgage stating that her husband—a man Leo has never met—was employed at the firm. She even went so far as impersonating someone from human resources on the *telephone—a clear case of fraud, something a lawyer like Alecia should know.*

Alecia was lucky that the partners didn't fire her when that happened—or press charges. In fact, it was Leo who had vouched for her and explained to everyone that she'd simply made a mistake and wasn't intentionally trying to commit fraud. Most of the partners wanted her terminated then, but Leo had argued that she would pull herself together and make a good employee.

He'd been wrong—and now it was his unenviable duty to finally let her go.

Just because the termination was warranted doesn't make it any easier. Leo's heart breaks for her. He knows her husband isn't working, which has put extra stress on her. And he really does believe that if she gets her act together she will make a good lawyer someday.

"I really do wish you the best," Leo says. "I think you can have a bright future if you live up to your potential."

With this statement, Alecia starts to cry.

"It's not fair," she says between sobs.

Leo says nothing in response, but, again, he is perplexed. He thinks he's been more than fair. It was him who gave her a second chance—she's the one who blew that second chance.

"I'll walk you to your desk so you can collect your things," Leo says, not knowing what else to say.

There's just no good way to deliver bad news. But Leo's done his best to treat Alecia with dignity and respect.

CHAPTER 42

ANDREW IS WAITING FOR Alecia outside in their *Honda. He spots her exiting the building, and he can see that she's carrying a cardboard box. As she gets closer to the Honda, he can see her more clearly. It looks like she's been crying—her eyes are puffy and red—but there's no sign of tears anymore. Her face is pinched with anger.*

"What happened?" Andrew says.

"That son of a bitch fired me!" Alecia snaps.

She opens the back hatch, tosses in the box of stuff from her desk, and slams the door with a boom that rocks the whole SUV. Andrew eases out of the car, trying not to put any strain on his back, and takes her by the shoulders.

Andrew has been on disability for two years from a back injury he suffered when he was in the army.

"They can't do that," Andrew says. "Who fired you?"

"My supervisor," Alecia says. "Leo Fisher."

"The guy who put you on probation?"

She nods.

"That asshole has always had it in for you," Andrew says, seething with anger.

"Don't I know it," she says, shaking her head.

"He said you're definitely fired?" Andrew asks.

"You saw the box of crap I carried out with me, didn't you? Leo practically hovered over my desk while I packed up my things. Did he think I was going to run off with my computer?"

"It's not over yet," Andrew says, and he starts across the parking lot toward the firm's entrance.

"Wait," Alecia says. "Don't do anything crazy."

But she doesn't follow him, or call him back. Part of her wants him to do something crazy. Part of her wants to do something crazy herself.

She's at the end of her rope after supporting both of them—and taking care of Andrew. He's on enough painkillers to tranquilize a horse, but it's still not enough. She's lucky if he's able to do a few chores around the house while she's at work. And the disability payments don't do enough to help their bottom line.

She's been at her wit's end for months now. What is she going to do without a job?

She's never felt so desperate in her life.

When she met Andrew in law school, it had seemed that the whole world was at their feet. After they were married five years ago, she became an immigration lawyer and he worked as a lawyer for the army. Life was good, full of promise. But two years ago Andrew slipped on a patch of ice during physical training and injured his back.

Their lives have been on a slow downward spiral ever since.

She waits in the car, sick with nervousness. She doesn't know what to expect. Andrew might be up there right now, appealing to Leo by explaining how he hasn't been able to work because of his back injury. A good lawyer knows that when logic and reason don't work with someone, an appeal to emotions could. Maybe Andrew could convince Leo to reconsider.

Or maybe Andrew is up there punching Leo in the nose. She half expects to hear police sirens and to see Andrew come running out, telling her to hit the gas.

A few minutes later, Andrew comes out, sauntering a bit. When he approaches, he has an ornery smirk on his face.

"What happened?" Alecia says. "Did you talk to him?"

"Nope," Andrew says, still grinning. "I just looked in his office window."

"What the hell are you smiling about then?"

"Because I've got an idea," Andrew says.

"What kind of idea?" Alecia asks, intrigued.

"Payback."

CHAPTER 43

"I CAN'T BELIEVE I ever listened to you," Alecia says, as she pulls the vehicle to a stop at another light.

"Me?" Andrew says, stuffing the last of his clothes into the garbage bag. "I just wanted to get some information about the company and use it to extort them. You're the one who wanted to kill him."

"Killing Leo was your idea," Alecia snaps.

"No it wasn't," Andrew roars, opening the cap on a bottle of ammonia and splattering the liquid onto the bloody clothes. "Murder wasn't on my radar until you brought it up."

Alecia opens her mouth to argue, but she notices a car pulling up behind them at the light.

It's a police cruiser.

"Shhhh," she hisses, looking forward and acting like nothing is wrong. "Cop!"

Andrew freezes. Seconds tick by and the light doesn't change. The two cars are the only ones at the intersection. The whole interior of their SUV reeks of ammonia.

When the light turns green, Alecia eases forward, making sure to obey the speed limit. The police car stays behind them, not turning on its lights but not passing them.

"They know," Andrew says. "Leo must have seen you."

"You can't know that. Don't freak out." She hesitates, thinking. "You said Leo was dead for sure."

"I thought he was. I cut his throat, for Christ's sake."

"Jesus, you're pathetic," Alecia mutters. "You can't get anything right."

The streets are practically empty, and there are plenty of opportunities for the police car to pass them or turn off, but it doesn't.

"He's running our plates right now," Andrew hisses.

"You're just being paranoid," Alecia says, but then she sees another police car approaching from the other direction.

"Damn it," she says, knowing that Andrew is right— they've been made.

The car behind them lights up like a Christmas tree. Alecia turns the corner and stomps on the gas. Both police cars pursue, sirens wailing.

Alecia races onto a busy thoroughfare, weaving in and out of cars. The police cruisers stay close behind. Tires squeal. Horns honk.

"I can't lose them," Alecia says.

More police cars appear from side streets. Alecia yanks the wheel and heads toward a shopping mall. It's closed for the night, and she thinks she might be able to outrun the cops through the empty parking lot. But more police cars race in from other entrances.

She slams the brakes and skids to a halt, one tire up on a grass median. A cloud of rubber smoke drifts through the headlight beams. The SUV shudders and stalls.

Police cars converge on their vehicle, officers exiting, shouting, drawing their guns.

"What do we do?" Andrew says, his voice a frightened whimper.

Alecia is a lawyer—she knows what happens next.

"We go to jail."

With that, she steps out of the car holding her hands high in the air.

A minute later, officers surround the SUV and pull Andrew out and handcuff him. As they do so, the officers exchange sideways glances, not sure what to think. This is a first for all of them.

Andrew Schmuhl is naked except for an adult diaper.

CHAPTER 44

LEO WAKES FROM A nightmare, gasping.

He looks around the hospital room, tries to orient himself. He can't seem to get enough air, so he reaches instinctively to his throat. An IV tube dangling from his arm restricts his movement. He tries with the other arm and finds a thick bandage wrapped around his neck.

The nightmare, he realizes, was not a dream.

He lived through it.

But did Sue?

He tries to sit up and finds he doesn't have the strength. The door opens, and Leo spots a doctor standing in the hallway, talking to a police officer. The detective is wearing plainclothes, but there is a gun visible on his hip. His attire seems legitimate—not at all like the getup Andrew Schmuhl was wearing when he came to the door.

"Five minutes," the doctor says to the officer. "He needs rest."

The detective walks into the room and looks compassionately at Leo.

"Sue?" Leo says, his voice barely more than a raspy whisper.

"I don't know," he says. "Sorry."

Leo closes his eyes, remembering the way the gunshot made Sue's hair blow out like it had been hit with a puff of air. He sees Andrew Schmuhl climbing on top of her, driving the knife down again and again. He opens his eyes again, hoping the images won't follow him into the real world.

"Leo," the officer says, grinning like a man who wants to deliver good news. "We got 'em. Alecia and Andrew Schmuhl are in custody as we speak."

"Good," Leo says, nodding. "That's good."

"Thanks to you," the detective says.

"Thanks to Sue," Leo says, swallowing hard. "I wouldn't be here if it wasn't for her."

Leo turns his head and begins crying.

"I'll leave you alone," the detective says. "We'll get a full statement from you later. I just wanted to let you know that the Schmuhls can't hurt you or anyone else anymore."

As the detective leaves, the doctor walks into Leo's room.

"Mr. Fisher," the doctor says, "your wife has just come out of surgery."

"Is she ...?"

The doctor nods.

"It's going to be a long recovery," he says, "but she's going to make it."

Leo lets out an audible sob.

"Would you like to see her?"

The doctor has a nurse bring in a wheelchair, and the two of them help him into it. As they push him down the hall, they wheel his IV stand along with him.

When they enter Sue's hospital room, Leo almost breaks down crying again.

There is an IV in her arm, an oxygen tube in her nose, a wire clipped to her finger that measures her heartbeat, and gauze dressings on her neck and the side of her head. Her skin is ghostly pale, but her chest is rising and falling unmistakably.

"Oh, Muffy," he says, his voice hoarse and gravelly.

He takes her hand. Her skin is cold. Leo is thankful for the steady *beep beep beep* of the heart rate monitor, reassuring him that she is alive.

"You were so brave," he whispers to her. "Come back to me."

He thinks about how he's taken life with Sue for granted. He's never been an absent husband. He's always enjoyed spending time with her rather than going out with friends. But he hasn't appreciated how precious their time together is—how easily their life together could be snatched away from them at any moment.

Sue's eyelids flicker for a moment, and then they open. Leo isn't sure she's awake until her eyes focus on his and recognition comes over her face.

"Oh, Muffy," he says, pressing his forehead against hers.

CHAPTER 45

Six months later

SUE PRESSES THE PREHEAT button on the oven.
Then she checks the two chicken breasts in a casserole
dish on the counter, soaking in marinade. There's nothing
more for her to do at the moment, so she sits down at the
kitchen table with Leo. Her husband has brought a book,
but it sits unopened on the table. Both Leo and Sue are
staring blankly, their minds elsewhere.

Even though they're following the same routine they
used to, nothing is the same for them these days. Sue still
cooks dinner, and Leo still sits at the table to keep her
company. But there's no joy in the experience anymore.
They don't banter like they once did. Leo rarely opens a
book, and when he does try to read, he finds his eyes drift-
ing over the words, not absorbing anything. And when
Sue makes dinner, she simply goes through the motions.
They don't eat much anyway. Leo has trouble chewing because of a severed nerve in his neck. Sue never has much
of an appetite.

Physically, they both suffer from permanent damage. Leo has a nasty scar on his neck and has trouble controlling his tongue. His injuries are hard on an attorney valued by his clients for his communication skills.

As for Sue, most of her scars are hidden beneath her clothes or—in the case of the groove carved into the side of her skull—her hair. But she suffers from chronic headaches and a ringing in her ears.

It's the wounds on the inside that hurt the most.

Every night, they lie awake, unable to sleep. And when they do finally fall asleep, they have nightmares.

Tonight, they're expecting a guest, but when the doorbell rings, both of them jump in their seats, remembering the chain of events on November ninth that began with the ringing of the doorbell.

Both Leo and Sue walk to the foyer and look through the spyhole before opening the door. Their guest, Casey Lingan, the chief deputy commonwealth's attorney prosecuting their case, greets them with handshakes and a smile.

Back in the kitchen, sitting at the table, the three of them discuss the upcoming trials of Andrew and Alecia Schmuhl.

"Everything looks good," Casey says. "We're charging them with abduction, burglary, use of a firearm, and aggravated malicious wounding. I feel confident that any jury will find these two guilty on most, if not all, charges."

The commonwealth's attorney explains that there will be two separate trials for Andrew and Alecia because the

Schmuhls are blaming each other. Alecia says she's a battered wife and that the whole thing was Andrew's idea. Andrew says he was out of his mind on pain medication and claims Alecia was the mastermind behind the crime.

"I don't think either of their excuses are going to hold up," the attorney says. "We've got plenty of evidence to poke holes in their stories."

Casey explains that there's video footage of Alecia purchasing the Taser and of Andrew buying the burner cell phones, showing both conspired to commit the crime. And while it's true that Andrew Schmuhl collected disability for a back injury and had prescriptions for enough painkillers to make a heroin addict as high as a kite, the commonwealth's attorney's office doesn't think the excuse will hold up.

"This guy has a dozen different prescriptions for back pain, high blood pressure, insomnia, incontinence," Casey says. "But we have eyewitnesses who saw him playing kickball last summer and repairing the roof of his mom's house two weeks before the attack."

"Sounds like you've got it all covered," Leo says, concentrating on his words because of the difficulty using his tongue now.

Leo knows an open-and-shut case when he sees one, but that doesn't make this experience any less stressful. He'll be worried until he hears a jury foreman say the word "guilty."

Sue has been quiet while they've talked, but now she clears her voice and asks, "What I still don't understand is what they were trying to accomplish? Why take us hostage? Why ask all those questions?" She swallows hard. "Why didn't he just come in and kill us?"

The lawyer is ready for this question—he expects jurors will want to know the same thing.

"We think they wanted to get some kind of information from Leo that they could use to extort money from the other firm partners," Casey explains. "Andrew Schmuhl's questions were vague because they didn't actually know what they were looking for. They wanted Leo to start blabbing, giving them all the dirt about the company. The only thing they weren't expecting—"

"There was no dirt," Leo says, finishing the sentence for him.

Sue frowns and shakes her head, still unable to believe what happened to them.

"One more thing," the attorney says. "We found notes in the Schmuhl's apartment with home information of several partners at the firm. It's possible they were going to do the same thing to other partners. You were just the first."

Leo reaches out and puts a hand on Sue's arm.

"You might have saved more lives than just ours, Muffy."

Sue rises, uncomfortable from the compliment, and puts the chicken in the oven. Leo walks Casey to the door and they shake hands.

"Keep us posted if there are any new developments," Leo says.

"Will do," the lawyer says. "Rest assured, the Schmuhls are going to be behind bars for a long time."

After Leo closes the door, he locks the deadbolt and arms their alarm system. When he returns to the kitchen, he finds Sue sitting at the table. He sits next to her. She offers him her best effort at a smile.

Both of their spirits are uplifted—a little bit, at least—by the visit. Twist and Shout stroll into the kitchen and purr for Leo and Sue to pet them.

"Maybe when the trials are over," Leo says, "our lives can go back to normal."

"I'd like that," Sue says, and now the smile on her face doesn't seem forced.

It warms Leo's heart to see her this way. Maybe they can be happy again.

The doorbell rings, and Leo and Sue both flinch at the noise. Their minds flash to memories of November ninth: the jolting electricity from the Taser's barbs, the report of the pistol and the smell of gun smoke, the sensation of the knife slicing into flesh.

"I'm sure it's just Casey," Leo says, his throat suddenly tight, his voice constricted. "He must have forgotten to tell us something."

Sue nods nervously.

"Probably," she says.

The doorbell rings again.

Leo imagines that every time the doorbell rings, for the rest of their lives, they'll be haunted by memories of what happened. He remembers Sue's strength on the night they were attacked.

Now, he realizes, he must be brave for her.

"Come on," he says, trying to sound confident as he reaches out and takes Sue's hand. "Let's do it together."

They rise and walk to the foyer. Leo peeks through the spyhole in the door and sees the blurry, distorted image of a man with his back to the door.

It could be Casey. But it might not be.

"We can't live in fear forever," Leo says.

Leo's hand is trembling as he wraps his fingers around the knob. Sue gives him a reassuring nod. He takes a deep breath and swings the door open.

MURDER
ON
THE RUN

PART ONE

CHAPTER 1

March 13, 2008
Omaha, Nebraska

CURSING UNDER HIS BREATH, he tried to correct his shaky aim. He knew he needed to seriously focus or he'd blow this one chance at cleanly eliminating the figure that was literally *right in front of him*. The shot could not be easier. He went to squeeze the trigger and—

Vooosh!

The high-pitched, deafening whine sprang up from out of nowhere, causing the boy to inadvertently shift his joystick.

"Aw, *man!*" he cried out in frustration. Of all times for the housekeeper, Shirlee, to fire up the vacuum cleaner! Taking advantage of the boy's flub, the Nazi on the TV screen leapt out from behind a bombed-out shack and tossed a grenade at a charging American tank. A massive loss of game points.

All day, eleven-year-old Tom Hunter had been jacked up knowing he would be coming home to his new Xbox and the latest version of *Call of Duty*. Though he was a top student, he had been distracted in every class by dreams of trudging through the fields of France along with the rest of the Allies. When school had finally let out, the slender, slightly gawky boy with oval-shaped eyeglasses had run right home from the bus. Grabbing one of the basement den's overstuffed sofa cushions, he'd firmly entrenched himself in front of the family TV.

Tom's older brothers were away at college, and it would be a while before his father got home from work at the hospital (and started asking about the untouched homework in Tom's backpack). For the next precious hour, the boy had the TV and one of the decisive battles of World War II all to himself. He just hadn't counted on interference from the civilian directly upstairs: Shirlee, who continued obliviously sawing the vacuum cleaner back and forth. Though Tom loved the portly, caring Shirlee, right now her kindness was forgotten and he felt only annoyance. Couldn't she have done her noisy cleaning while he was at school?

Gritting his teeth, Tom prepared to refocus his aim when—incredibly—the doorbell buzzed.

"No *way!*" he roared. He tried to ignore the sound and gripped the controller tighter. But, again, the buzzer ricocheted through the huge house—this time more insistently.

"*Shirlee!*" Tom cried. "Can you get that? *Please!*"

At last, the vacuum cleaner mercifully stopped and Tom heard Shirlee's tired tread as she walked to the front door. Turning his attention back to the game, Tom repositioned himself but then immediately heard loud voices. It sounded like some kind of argument, and then someone shouted. Heavy footsteps began walking back and forth overhead.

Suddenly, a loud thump of the floor was followed by a strange sound—a kind of muffled cry.

The boy cocked his head and listened. Frowning, he put his joystick down and then he heard another odd sound—almost like someone clearing their throat. And although it wasn't a spoken word, Tom knew immediately that it was Shirlee. And that something was wrong—seriously wrong.

Tom stood and quietly went up the stairs. He paused at the top. Now, he didn't hear a thing except for the game's noises downstairs. But then he turned to look down the main hallway.

A man was standing there, a small man that Tom didn't know. And he wasn't exactly standing, he was swaying in the hall outside of the kitchen. His eyes were red-rimmed and very black, and his face was streaked with sweat although it was a mild spring day. Though Tom had never seen one in real life, his immediate thought was that this was a drunk person. A drunk man in a dirty coat was standing in the middle of his house!

Tom was so astonished he almost laughed. But then he saw Shirlee.

Kind, caring Shirlee—lying in a crumpled heap at the man's feet. Blood everywhere.

And then he saw the knife in the man's hand.

The scream that Tom let out seemed to startle the intruder, who blinked several times in rapid succession. In a flash, Tom bolted toward the front door—he was there almost before he was even conscious of running.

The man hurled his body forward and grabbed Tom's shoulder. He yanked the boy backward and took a crushing grip of the top of his head. He roughly steered Tom into the dining room.

Tom yelped in panic. *WHAT was happening?* As he struggled, the man shoved him against the sleekly polished dining room table. The boy cried out, "*HEL*—"

His cry was cut off as the man's hands went over his mouth. Tom fought wildly, grunting and twisting his body to and fro, trying to knock things off of the table. Through his terror and shock, he suddenly felt something hard and cold press against his throat. Then, strange spots began dancing in front of his eyes.

A wave of darkness started to wash over him. Through it, Tom was dimly aware that—off in a distance that seemed impossibly far away—the noisy Xbox effects coming from the television had abruptly stopped.

His game was over. The battle had been lost.

CHAPTER 2

LATER, HE WOULD WISH that something had looked wrong from the outside of the house. Some alarming telltale sign—a shattered window pane, the front door gaping open, a maroon stain on the front step—*anything* that might have helped prepare him.

But as the blue twilight fell and Dr. William Hunter pulled up to his two-story brick house, everything looked perfect, particularly its impeccably manicured lawn. All of the residents of the historic Dundee neighborhood took pride in keeping up their homes' appearance, and the Hunters were no different. As the doctor glanced appreciatively over the front of the house, the only element out of place was the red Taurus parked in the driveway: Shirlee's car. What was she still doing there, he wondered with a look at the dashboard clock. It was just after five p.m., and Shirlee usually left promptly at four thirty, as she had her own family to attend to.

The doctor sighed with mild exasperation. If Tom had

made that poor overworked woman stay late to make him something special for dinner, he'd have to have a talk with his son. *And* with his housekeeper; she indulged the boy far too much. But as he got out of his car, Hunter found that he was smiling. He knew damned well that he was often just as guilty of giving in to Tom. How could he not? Tom had been an unexpected child, eight years younger than his nearest brother; it was almost inevitable that he would be a tad spoiled. Plus, he was simply a fantastic kid. Tom's energy and enthusiasm for *everything* kept his white-haired and bearded fifty-five-year-old father feeling young.

Dr. Hunter opened the front door and glanced down at the elaborately carved console table; a stack of mail was piled on the glossy marble top. As he casually flicked through the bills and advertisements, the tinny sound of gunfire mixed with bombastic music suddenly came up from the basement. Tom was clearly playing a video game instead of doing his homework.

"Hey, Tom!" Hunter yelled from the hall. "Can ya pause the Normandy invasion and say hello to your tired dad?"

There was no response, just that same gunfire and music. It stopped for a moment, then started right back up. It seemed to be on a loop, as though the game was stuck on its program menu. The repetition was irritating.

"Hey, Tom, come on!" Hunter yelled again. Shuffling the bills, he turned slightly and almost walked into the vacuum cleaner that was standing in the middle of the hallway. *How very unlike Shirlee to have just left it here,* he

thought. *Sloppy, even.* Hunter liked a tightly run home. He might really have to have a talk with his housekeeper after all.

Heading toward the kitchen, Hunter's gaze was caught by something up ahead at the end of the hallway: a dark pool of some kind of liquid. Now what was *that*? A spilled cola? Why hadn't it been cleaned up?

"Shirlee!" he called out. "Hey, what's going on around—"

As he approached, he saw that there were more stains, a spray of them across the walls.

And on the floor lay Shirlee Sherman, facedown, covered in blood.

Hunter gasped and froze on the spot.

It was only the video game music starting up again that startled him into panic.

Tom. *Where is Tom?*

He pivoted around and inadvertently stepped on something that gave a loud crunch. He moved his foot and saw that they were oval-shaped glasses.

Tom's glasses.

Hunter lunged toward the basement door, but before he got there his eye was caught by something off to the side in the dining room.

He saw it was another body.

He saw that it was his son.

His eleven-year-old son, Thomas Hunter.

The images came in such quick succession they almost knocked the doctor over. It was too much to take in all at once, yet he had no choice. He had to process that he was standing in the hallway of his home staring at the bent over body of his son.

Hunter raced over and dropped to his knees. He grabbed Tom's wrist and desperately started checking for a pulse, but some part of him—the pathologist with decades of experience behind him—was fully aware that the boy was dead.

And then, an instant later, he saw the awful confirmation of that fact.

On the other side of his son's throat, sticking out at an almost perfect forty-five-degree angle, was a long, glinting kitchen knife.

CHAPTER 3

EVERY FACE IN THE crowd turned to look and then stare—some stared with curiosity, some with suspicion, many with fear.

Detective Derek Mois was used to it. A craggily handsome man with short copper-colored hair and a weightlifter's neck, Mois's physical presence commanded attention. He was often called "Jarhead" by his friends, even though he hadn't served in the military. He didn't mind; it was a useful front when dealing with unruly mobs and potential suspects. And the tattoos on both of his forearms provided good backup.

Mois wove his unmarked car past the gaping onlookers and television camera vans. He couldn't help but compare this crime scene to those he'd seen in Omaha's lesser neighborhoods. Even the prospect of a juicy murder rarely lured all three local TV stations out to the dicier areas. And most of the time, the residents were too afraid to come out and see what was happening. Or, they just didn't want to get involved. There had been five murders in Omaha already that year, but none had occurred in an upscale suburb like this one.

Probably for that very reason, it looked like nearly every resident of the historic district was milling about in front of Dr. William Hunter's home. Mois had to steer around five flashing patrol cars and two ambulances huddled closely together in front of the house. The usually tranquil neighborhood was so congested that the closest available parking spot was four doors down.

Walking back up the street, it seemed to Mois that this crowd's mood was almost festive. Everyone gathered on the street was excitedly talking, mostly on top of each other.

"It was a burglary, right?"

"We've been overdue. The last robbery I can remember in Dundee was in 2005."

"No, that guy over there said this is a domestic abuse situation."

"*William and Claire Hunter?* Are you crazy? They're doctors, for goodness sake!"

"They're married, aren't they? Even doctors can fight."

"No, no—it's something to do with one of the boys. A drug overdose."

Mois ruefully shook his head. So much misinformation out there, and it spread so quickly nowadays thanks to the Internet and smartphones.

The police had cordoned off the perimeter around the house, but one of the junior officers recognized the detective with a nod and let him through. Lights blazed out of the house's graceful front windows; Mois thought the scene looked as lit up as a movie premiere. A balding, jowly cop with a thick gray mustache was guarding the door.

"Hey, Matt," Mois said. "Big night, huh?"

"Big understatement," the older man replied with a snort. "It's like election night at the governor's mansion."

Mois looked over the elegantly appointed home. "Swanky digs. What do we have? Hedge-fund manager take a bullet from a pissed off investor?"

"Nah, this one's bad, Mois," the cop said with a deep sigh. "Middle-aged woman and a kid, no more than ten years old."

"*Here?*" Mois exclaimed. "What, some kind of family dispute?"

"No idea," Matt shrugged. "They don't tell me nuthin'."

Clapping the other man on the shoulder, Mois entered the house. A swarm of officers and technicians were clustered together at the end of a long hallway. Mois approached and saw that the group was surrounding a short, stout woman curled up on the floor in a near fetal position. She looked to be in her late fifties and was wearing hot pink sweat pants and a light blue shirt, now accented with splashes of bright red blood.

Bending over the body was a petite woman in her mid-thirties wearing a face mask and plastic gloves. She glanced up through her stylish designer glasses at Mois and beckoned with a nod of her head for him to crouch down next her.

"Dr. Allen," Mois said formally. He'd encountered medical examiner Jane Allen on a few crime scenes and recalled that she was all business, all the time.

"Good evening, Detective," the doctor answered back just as formally. "Victim number one: Shirlee Sherman, housekeeper. Discovered by the homeowner, William Hunter, a doctor and professor at Creighton University. He's outside."

With a furrowed brow, Mois leaned in closer and noted that the bloodstains were concentrated around the woman's upper body. In the middle of her throat, a long knife had been stuck nearly to the hilt.

"All the wounds are in her neck?" he asked.

Dr. Allen nodded. "At least ten. We'll get the exact number at the autopsy. Looks like killer was aiming for the carotid artery."

Mois let out a low whistle. "Brutal, leaving the knife in the body like that. Haven't seen that signature before."

"Well, you're about to see it again," Dr. Allen said curtly as she stood up and removed her face mask. "The second victim is in the dining room."

As the two moved away from the cluster, the detective glanced down and saw a yellow evidence marker on the floor; it pointed to a pair of broken eyeglasses—so small that they had to belong to a child.

"Brace yourself," Dr. Allen warned, seeing Mois pause at the chilling sight. "It doesn't get much worse than this."

CHAPTER 4

DR. ALLEN'S POINT WAS well taken.

Though Mois had seen plenty of gruesome murder scenes, this one seemed both savage *and* coolly executed.

The boy was twisted over on his side, facedown on the rug. In his shorts and striped T-shirt, he looked like pretty much any other skinny, slightly awkward preadolescent boy. In fact, Mois was immediately struck by how much Tom Hunter resembled his own son, Danny. Though there was a pool of blood to one side of the body, the wounds visible on the child's throat looked eerily neat and precise. The savage aspect was the glinting knife sticking out from the child's neck; to Mois, it looked like a macabre Halloween costume prosthetic.

"Five wounds total," Dr. Allen said. "Same location."

"Who could do this to a *kid*?" Mois wondered with disgust.

Dr. Allen gave a small, bitter shrug.

As a group of technicians took swabs off the corpse and

a photographer documented the area, Mois looked back and forth at the position of Tom's body relative to the housekeeper's.

"So...it looks like the killer came in from the back of the house and attacked the housekeeper first?" he asked.

"Got me; that's your area," the examiner said. "But it seems more likely the killer came in by the front door. The vacuum cleaner was in the middle of the hall, like the housekeeper was cleaning when he entered. No signs of forced entry in either the back or front, so it's probable she let him in."

"Or the boy let him in," Mois countered.

"Mmmm. He was playing a video game in the basement. Would your son leave his game to answer the door?"

Mois gave a rueful nod. "Good point. So...if he came in the front, he would have had to make his way to the kitchen to get the knives. Maybe he came through the front door without either of them being aware?"

They both mused on the possibilities for a moment. Then Mois asked, "In whatever order, why *kill* an eleven-year-old boy and a middle-aged woman? Any signs of sexual assault on either?"

"Doesn't look like it. I'll show you the basement."

Mois and Dr. Allen again walked past the housekeeper's body. As they moved down the hall, Mois noted the opulent home's luxurious silk drapes and gold-flecked embossed wallpaper. He couldn't help but wonder how much a house like this listed for.

Glancing into the kitchen, Mois saw another yellow evidence marker: an expensive-looking knife set was prominently displayed on the counter. Two knives were missing. Allen nodded toward them.

"It doesn't look like the killer came prepared for attack. He used what he could find. But there aren't any signs of ransacking," Dr. Allen said with puzzlement. "And the housekeeper's purse was sitting on the counter right there. With eight hundred dollars in her wallet."

She opened a hallway door and they went down into the basement. It was a comfortably furnished den with a big sofa and two leather club chairs. Yet another technician was at work. She lifted a dismantled Xbox console from the television and placed it carefully into a plastic evidence bag.

"The rest of the house is just as immaculate as this room," Dr. Allen noted. "Looks like Mrs. Sherman was just about finished with her work..."

Mois took it all in and then, with a long, pained sigh, turned to Dr. Allen. She gave him a knowing nod—this time it was just a little less businesslike.

"You can only put it off for so long," she said sympathetically.

"Yeah... Time to talk to the father."

CHAPTER 5

DR. HUNTER KEPT TRYING to look away from the bloodstains on his hands. And on his shirt. And on his pants. He forced himself to stare at the red and blue flashing lights on top of the police cars but, eventually, his gaze would drop back down.

As he sat in the back of an ambulance, a paramedic tried to put a blanket over his shoulders. He shrugged it off. It wouldn't help. There was nothing the paramedics could do, there was nothing anyone could do.

His beloved youngest son, Tom, had been brutally attacked and was lying inside the house, dead. This was the cold hard fact. And the only thing Hunter could do was try to find some way to accept that awful reality and make some sense of it—an impossible task.

His wife, Claire, had been away on an "alone time" holiday in Hawaii. He had imagined her coming back relaxed, happy, her skin tanned and glowing. Her time swimming in the ocean might have given her light-brown hair some honey-colored streaks. What would she look like when she got off the plane now?

"Dr. Hunter?"

A man stood in front of him. A handsome, tough-looking man.

"I'm Detective Derek Mois," he said. Hunter thought that this guy had a real take-control kind of look, which gave the doctor a sudden jolt of hope—though just what there was to hope for at this point he couldn't say.

"I'm so sorry for your loss," Mois said as he shook Hunter's hand and then, surprising the doctor, gently placed his other hand over their grasp. "Is your wife here?"

"She's on her way back from Hawaii. I called her with the...I told her what happened. Have you learned anything yet?" Hunter asked, his voice rising. "I mean—who did this? Why? How could this have happened to *us*?"

The doctor's face went red and he could feel his shock finally giving way to anger—or rather, fury.

"We've got a lot of good people—experts in their fields—examining the scene," Mois said with calming authority. "And they'll be able to tell us a great deal in the coming days. I know you want answers, but right now I've got to ask you a lot of questions. I'm sorry, I know it's painful."

"Of course, yes—anything I can tell you," Hunter said in a desperate voice.

Mois briskly pulled out his notebook but, realizing he needed to ease into this, paused and took a seat on the back of the ambulance next to the doctor.

"Why don't you start by telling me about Tom?" he suggested. "What did he like to do? Who were his friends?"

William Hunter just stared at the ground for a long, uncomfortable beat.

"I—I'm sorry," he said with choked, renewed shock. "It's just—hearing him referred to in the past tense. I guess we have to get used to that..."

The doctor then cleared his throat and began talking quickly, as if it were the best way to keep his emotions in check. "Tom's in the sixth grade, a great student. Pretty much straight A's. His favorite subjects are—*were* math and science. He played soccer and basketball at the YMCA. He loved video games, chatting with friends online. He had a lot of friends, the whole neighborhood..."

Hunter's torrent of words trailed off; he seemed at loss as to what else to say or how to say it. After a moment, he said quietly, "He loved chili fries. They were his favorite food."

There was another long, painful silence, the doctor clearly overwhelmed with grief. Mois gave him a moment, then stood up and faced him. "Can you think of a reason why anyone would enter your house? Are you known to keep a lot of money in the house? Do you owe money?"

Mois knew this his abrupt change of topic was a risk but it worked. The blunt questions seemed to throw the doctor a lifeline, it gave him something to address directly.

"No, no I don't!" Hunter said empathically. "I don't keep cash in the house. Or guns. Or prescription drugs. I don't gamble. I have no debts, no unstable family members. Claire doesn't give a damn about jewelry. They could have taken *whatever* they wanted from the house—I don't care! Why did they have to *kill* my boy?"

"We'll find out. I assure you we'll do everything we can to get to the bottom of this," Mois said gravely. "What about your housekeeper, Shirlee? Ever had concerns about her or her family members?"

"No!" Dr. Hunter said in a shocked tone. "Shirlee's been with us for years—she's a grandmother. She's one of the most responsible people I've ever known."

"Even perfectly responsible folks can get involved with the wrong people or...activities. Mrs. Sherman had over eight hundred dollars in her purse," Mois said. "That's a lot of cash to be carrying around. Do you know why she would have that much?"

Hunter shook his head helplessly. "No...no, I don't know. Was nothing taken from the house?"

"It doesn't look like it, but we'll need you to look around and give us a definitive answer on that," Mois said. "And I'm afraid we're going to have to remove some items. Like Tom's computer. It might give us some information. Kids these days have a whole online life that we parents don't really know about."

Hunter sighed. "Whatever you need. His books, his games, his phone. It doesn't matter. It's all just stuff. The only thing we care about has already been taken from us."

As the doctor fought to tamp down another rising sob, a fit man in a blue Nike track suit warily approached the back of the ambulance. He gave Hunter a look of pained concern.

"I'm—I'm so sorry, Bill," he said haltingly to Hunter. "I—I can't imagine...I'm just so sorry."

Hunter nodded appreciatively but seemed unable to speak. Seeing his distress, the man turned to face Mois.

"My name is Paul Medlin. I live three houses down," he said anxiously. "And I think I saw something."

CHAPTER 6

THE KNIVES STICKING OUT of the victims' throats.

Mois couldn't get the images out of his mind. Even as he busily filled out the endless forms related to the murders, those shiny pieces of polished metal flashed in front of him.

He shook his head to refocus and attacked the paperwork with renewed vigor. There was always so much to do, so many possible leads to follow up, never enough time to do it all. Mois was soon so deep in thought that he didn't even notice Sergeant Teresa Negron standing in his office doorway.

With her flawless mocha complexion and huge brown eyes, the sergeant could easily have been a runway model—were it not for her petite five foot four stature. She was often teased about her chic wardrobe; today, a butter-smooth tan suede jacket, black jeans, and killer heels. But her stylish appearance belied a serious do-not-even-*think*-of-messing-with-me vibe.

"*Ahem*—you need to get home, pardner," she finally said.

Mois nodded without looking up. "You hear about the Dundee killings?"

"Murkowski filled me in on the basics. I'm trying to close out the Sanders case. Lots of homework tonight," Negron said as she shifted under the weight of the Prada bag slung over her shoulder and the stack of files clutched to her chest. Since she had moved into Mois's division a few months earlier, the two had developed a rapport. Checking in at the end of their shifts had become a habit.

"By the way, Mois, you *do* know it's nearly nine o'clock, right?"

The detective glanced at the wall clock. He'd promised his wife, Lisa, that he'd try be home in time to at least say good night to their son even if he couldn't always join the family for dinner. And after what he had seen earlier that evening, it seemed extra important to keep to that vow.

As Mois started to hurriedly collect his things, Jim Murkowski—an intense-looking cop with a thatch of dark red hair—stuck his head in the door.

"Quick update," Murkowski said. "An officer on the Dundee scene talked to a neighbor. Says he saw a 'strange' car driving up and down the street at least twice this afternoon."

"How was it 'strange'?" Mois asked. "Rap music thumping? Nude chicks on the mudflaps?"

"Ha-ha. No, just a silver or gray SUV," the younger cop said. "It was strange to this guy because he didn't recognize it as a neighbor's. I guess these people keep close tabs on who comes into their hood."

"Good," Mois said. "Civic snobbery may be useful in this case. Don't suppose he noticed the license plates?"

"No luck there," Murkowski said as he ducked back out into the hall.

"A car description, that's something, anyway," Negron observed.

"We got a physical description, too," Mois reported. "A neighbor walking his dog saw a strange *man* in the hood. An 'odd, dark-haired, olive-skinned' man wandering around—stumbling, possibly drunk. Seemed lost or like he was looking for an address."

"Hmmm, *olive* skinned?" Negron asked. "Hispanic? Middle Eastern? Greek?"

"Dunno. I sent a sketch artist over," Mois said, grabbing his coat. "Be here eight thirty sharp tomorrow, we got a lot to go over."

"You might say 'please' once in a while, pardner," Negron said with mock testiness.

"*Please!*" Mois shouted over his shoulder—and then nearly ran into a woman in an aqua-colored health care jumper being escorted down the hall by Murkowski. The younger cop gave Mois a "heads-up" nod as he presented the woman, who had red-rimmed eyes and was clearly distressed.

"Detective Mois, this is Kelly Wedgewood, Shirlee Sherman's daughter," Murkowski explained. "She was good enough to come down and give us some information on her mother. Sergeant Blake thought you'd like to meet her."

Mois darted a glance at Negron, then the wall clock.

Though he hesitated for a moment, Mois knew this would have to be one of those nights when Danny wouldn't see his father.

"Of course, thank you for coming in," Mois said as he put down his case. He did a quick inventory of Kelly Wedgewood's appearance: pale skin, straw-colored hair that hadn't been styled in a while, a permanently tired-looking face. This was a woman who probably worked as hard as her mother had.

"I really can't stay," Kelly said with a catch in her throat. "I want to help, but my daughter is at a friend's and she's very scared and upset. She—she loved my mom so much."

"Ms. Wedgewood has given us a lot of background on Mrs. Sherman," Murkowski said. "No arrest record, no history of drug use, no sign of connections to criminal activities of any kind."

"I don't know why anyone would do this!" Kelly gasped, fighting back tears. "My mom has *five* grandchildren. She never thinks of herself, only others. She works literally every day of the week."

Mois nodded sympathetically then hesitated a moment. He knew he had to pose his next question carefully.

"Your mother had a great deal of cash in her purse. Can you think of a reason why?"

As renewed tears welled up in her eyes, Kelly wiped them with the back of her hand. Negron stepped forward with a box of tissues.

"That's probably just the rent money," Kelly said. "She

owns a small apartment building. It's not in a very good area. Most tenants pay in cash. Sometimes even in coin rolls."

"Has she ever had any disagreements with her tenants over money? Or maybe complaints about noise, fighting?" Mois asked.

"Not really. They're mostly undocumented immigrants; they don't look for trouble," Kelly said with a glance at the door, clearly aching to leave.

After a few more questions, Mois assured the woman that she'd been a big help and Murkowski escorted her out. Negron gave Mois a wry frown.

"Not a lot to go on, huh?" she said.

"None of this makes a *bit* of sense!" Mois exclaimed. "It wasn't a burglary gone wrong. It wasn't a home invasion by some meth head. Apparently, this was a deliberate killing. Someone purposefully came to that house today to kill two of the most vulnerable and blameless victims imaginable: an eleven-year-old boy and a grandmother. What possible motive could there be?"

Under Mois's frustration, Negron detected uncharacteristic anger.

"It happened, so there has to be a reason, Mois," she said reassuringly. "And we're going to do our job and we will eventually find out *who* and *why*. But you may miss a few 'good nights' with your son."

"Yeah," Mois sighed in agreement. "And I'm getting off easy. The Hunters are looking at a lifetime of missed nights…"

CHAPTER 7

MOIS MARVELED AT HOW burglars pulled off their stealth.

Not wanting to wake anyone, he had gently unlocked the front door and tried to quietly step into the foyer of his home. Instantly, the door let out a screaming whine and a floorboard moaned painfully. Some nights you just can't win, Mois thought.

A light was on down the hall in the kitchen. Mois figured Lisa had left out some dinner (and probably a terse note reminding him of his broken promise). As he walked past the darkened family den, he saw Danny was seated cross-legged playing a video game. The boy was silhouetted by the TV screen; the earphones clamped onto his small head were so comically oversized it looked as though they were attacking him. The thought amused Mois, until the horrific crime scene from earlier in the evening came back at him.

He tapped his son on the shoulder. Danny looked up

with a quick smile but quickly turned his attention back to his game. Frowning, Mois pulled off the kid's earphones—chaotic music and shrill game sound effects poured out.

"What are you still doing up?"

"Hold on, Dad! I'm beating Charlie!" Danny said in a loud stage whisper. *"And Mom's asleep so keep it down."*

Mois plopped onto the sofa behind Danny and watched as his son maneuvered through a battle of animated monsters. He'd attempted to play a game or two with Danny in the past, but the pace was just too frenetic and the scoring system completely bewildering. As his son shifted his body around to match his screen moves, Mois was struck again by Danny's resemblance to Tom Hunter: slender, nerdy oval-framed glasses, even wearing a striped T-shirt.

Finally, Danny either scored a major victory or was blown all to hell—it was difficult for Mois to tell which—and tore off his earphones.

"Why are you still up?" Mois asked again.

"Mom said I could till you got home—long as it was before ten thirty."

"Was she mad?"

"Naw," Danny said with a yawn. "She heard something bad happened today and said you'd be working late. She wouldn't tell me about it. Even though she *knows* I can just look it up online."

Mois smiled; it was like Lisa to figure he'd need to see his son this night. He felt a pang of guilt at thinking she might nag about his lateness.

Suddenly, a dialogue box popped up on the TV screen. Seeing it, Danny quickly typed back a message: "LOSER!"

"What are you doing? Who's that?" Mois asked.

"I told ya, Charlie. He's pissed that I won. *Again!*"

"Charlie from Little League? What's he doing up so late?" Mois asked, hating himself for sounding like an uptight and uncool parent.

"It's not *that* late. Matt's playing, too."

Mois thought for a moment. "Hey, tell me something: say you and Charlie wanted to talk privately—without Matt listening in—while all three of you were playing. Is that possible?"

"Dad, you'd do that mostly on a computer," Danny said impatiently, adults' tech ignorance always a trial to him. "There are online public and private chatrooms, and you can talk to whoever you want. Long as they want to talk to you. But yeah, if you're playing Xbox with your friends, and don't want to get up, you can use Xbox Live chat."

A number of scenarios ran through Mois's mind. He quickly took out his cell phone but, with a glance a Danny, kept it in the palm of his hand.

"Okay, up to bed, sport."

Mois watched as Danny methodically put away his game and quietly closed the TV cabinet doors. As Danny headed out, he turned to look at his father.

"How bad was it today, Dad?" the boy asked in a hushed voice.

Mois paused. He rarely shared the details of his job with Danny; he wanted his son to have a childhood, to be unaware of the potential horrors out there for as long as possible. But it was 2008, a different world; Danny probably knew a lot more than Mois had at his age.

"Very bad, Dan," Mois answered.

"Yeah...I kinda thought so," Danny said with concern. He gave Mois a small smile. "Love you, Dad."

Touched, Mois gave his son a wink and a thumbs-up. When the boy was out of the room, he again took out his phone. He hit Negron's number and, as it rang, he went out into the kitchen.

"*Really?*" the sergeant immediately complained. "I literally just walked in the door. It's nearly eleven o'clock!"

"Yeah, sorry, but I've got a potential angle I gotta run by you," Mois said excitedly. "My son tells me that online video gamers—people who don't know anything about each other—can chat while playing. Perfect setup for a predator to cultivate a relationship, right? Maybe a pedophile met Tom Hunter online and tracked him down."

There was a silent pause while Negron turned the idea over.

"Interesting," she said. "It fills in your motive blank. But wouldn't the guy have tried to meet up with the kid somewhere else? Coming to the house in the afternoon was a big risk—why would he assume the boy would be home alone?"

"Maybe Tom told him he would be after the housekeeper left. Remember, this guy could have posed as someone Tom's own age," Mois said, pacing the kitchen.

Negron was silent for another moment. "Well . . . let's get IT to dig into the boy's computer. I think they can cross-reference anyone he played online games with against anyone he met in a chat room. We'll have to see if the kid had a cell phone, too."

"Yep, do it. First thing in the morning, okay?" Mois demanded.

More silence came from Negron, more pointed this time.

"Sorry," Mois sighed. *"Please."*

"You got it, pardner."

CHAPTER 8

"FIFTEEN CUTS ON THE neck. See here? They form a pattern starting on the left front side."

The coroner tilted Shirlee Sherman's head to show the path of incisions along the dead woman's neck.

Mois was surprised at how detached this technician— Dr. Thad Chen—was acting, considering his youth. He looked like a college kid, what with the skinny jeans he wore under his lab coat and his hipster haircut—shorn on the sides, long on the top. But Mois thought Chen already had the seen-it-all demeanor of an older, more experienced technician. Then again, Mois mused, detachment was probably essential to this particular job.

"*Fifteen* cuts?" Mois asked. "That almost doesn't seem possible. Or, well, necessary."

"Yeah, he used just about all the real estate he could find," the coroner dryly noted. "The cuts get wider as they progress and finally culminate in this big C-shaped puncture."

"But why so many?" Mois asked as he jotted a note onto a small pad.

"No idea. He probably got the job done on the second or third incision. Same with the kid," Chen gestured over to the other gurney where Tom Hunter was laid out. "Five stab wounds in his neck, both his jugular vein and carotid arteries severed. It's almost as if the killer poked around specifically for those veins. It's almost surgical."

The lab room was chilly and various chemical odors seemed to be competing for dominance. Mois thought of poor Kelly Wedgewood having to identify her mother's body down here. The sterility of the autopsy room always made death seem unreal to Mois. In the buzzy fluorescent lighting, the yellowed cadavers often looked fake, like poorly made-up extras in a low-budget zombie movie.

"You think the killer has some kind of medical background? Or at least some level of physiological knowledge?" Mois wondered.

"Seems possible. There's deliberation here," the coroner noted. "In a normal assault, a killer would just slash across the throat if that was his target. Whoever did this went about it methodically, even though we can assume the victims were struggling. The boy has compression bruises around his mouth, probably from the killer muzzling him."

Mois contemplated the information then closed his pad and turned to go. The morgue gave him the willies; he didn't like to linger. But Dr. Chen held up his hand.

"Yo, there's something else I want to tell you," he said as he crossed over to his desk. He picked up a file and leafed through it. "You know the killer left knives in both of the victims' necks. A crazy strange MO, but *not* the first time I've seen it."

Mois stopped in his tracks. "Are you serious?"

"People tell me I'm always serious, too serious," Chen shrugged. "Anyway, just six months ago, a woman was stabbed to death in East Omaha. Her boyfriend found her, facedown, inside the front doorway of her home."

Chen slowly shook his head back and forth as he reviewed the file. Mois frowned with impatience.

"Yeah? *And?*" the detective asked.

The coroner looked up with a pained grimace, his first display of actual emotion.

"And the killer left *two* knives in the back of her head."

Mois was stunned. "Who was she?"

A voice spoke up suddenly behind the detective.

"Joy Blanchard," Sergeant Teresa Negron said tersely from the lab doorway. "And I know who killed her."

CHAPTER 9

"HOW COULD MURKOWSKI *NOT* have told me about the knives left in the bodies?" Negron fumed as she strode ahead of Mois out of the mortuary lab, her heels clacking angrily down the tile hallway. The steel-gray power suit she happened to put on that morning somehow lent authority to her fury.

"Calm down," Mois said as he moved to catch up with her. "He probably didn't know. I wanted to keep a lid on that detail for as long as possible out of respect to the families. And to weed out any crazy false confessions."

They came to the building exit, and Negron gave the double doors an irritated shove. Outside it was a muggy, overcast spring day. As the two headed toward the parking lot, a heavy roll of thunder sounded in the distance.

"And you weren't even officially on the case until this morning," Mois reminded her.

"Didn't stop you from calling me at eleven last night!" Negron said testily as she fumbled with a file she was carrying. She took a moment to calm herself. "Look, I get all this, Mois. It's just that the Blanchard case *really* burned me."

Stopping in front of her fire-red Mustang, the sergeant pulled out a photo from the file—a color mug shot—and held up it up directly to Mois's face.

"Feast your eyes," she said. "Craig Talley. Thirty-six years old. Dark hair. *Olive*-toned skin."

Mois took the photograph and let out a slow whistle. "*Damn*. This guy matches the Dundee killer's description like he was sent directly from Central Casting. What happened with the case?"

Negron let out a bitter laugh.

"Oh, we arrested him, but the DA—in all her wisdom—refused to file," she said scornfully. "Plenty of circumstantial evidence but not enough physical. So, the bastard walked."

The first drops of rain began to fall. One landed directly on the photo Mois was holding, leaving a stream of water running diagonally across Craig Talley's terse, angry-looking face.

"So, we're taking this to Chief Wolkoff, right?" Negron asked with a *do-not-disappoint-me* tone.

An even louder roll of thunder seemed to release the pent-up rain—it came down in a sudden deluge. Negron quickly clicked her car doors open and the two jumped inside.

As the water landed in a heavy drumbeat on the roof of the car, Mois turned to his partner. "Look, I know you're ready to speed dial Wolkoff with this, but we aren't there yet."

"We have a possible serial killer on the loose!" she objected.

"*Possible*," Mois noted. "But before we run this any further up, I want to find out more about this Talley. Is he even still *in* Omaha? What's the connection to the Hunters? And, by the way, does he fit a pedophile profile?"

Negron hesitated for a moment. The windows of the car were already steaming up—she took a frustrated wipe across the driver's side glass.

"No. Joy Blanchard was fifty-eight," she admitted. "But that's just a theory, anyway."

"Agreed, but we gotta check things off—one at a time."

Negron sighed impatiently but nodded in agreement. "You're right. But Jesus I hope we can nail this Talley guy. He is so *clearly* guilty. It kills me that he's still out there."

She stabbed her foot on the gas pedal and revved her car engine. "Where do we start?"

Thoughtfully rubbing his chin, Mois took another look at the mug shot.

"Let's get Murkowski to track down this guy's last whereabouts," he said. "Meanwhile, we're going to take this photo to Dr. Hunter. Let's see if it either introduces him to or *reacquaints* him with Mr. Craig Talley."

CHAPTER 10

ONE MURDER CAN TAKE so many lives.

The thought ran through Mois's mind as he looked at Dr. William Hunter. The man had aged a decade in the last forty-eight hours. He looked gaunt, hollowed out; like some essential energy force had been bled from him. Mois had seen the look before. He thought it likely that, from now on, the doctor would just be going through the motions of his life.

Mois and Negron tentatively entered Dr. Hunter's small, meticulously organized office at Creighton University, a sprawling campus with an attached medical facility. Hunter was sitting at his desk, staring down at some piece of paperwork, clearly not reading it—not even seeing it.

Across the desk was a thin middle-aged woman with pertly cut brown hair wearing a white lab coat; she had the same air of shell shock that Dr. Hunter had. Next to her was an older, spry-looking man with receding gray hair, also in a white lab coat. The three were sitting in silence, but the man jumped up when he heard Mois and Negron enter.

"Detectives?" he said with a warm, open smile—but a telltale crease of concern in his forehead. "Bill told me you were coming in this morning, so I thought I'd, well...I'd keep company till you arrived. I'm Dr. Roger Brumback."

Introductions were made, the woman identified as Claire Hunter, also a doctor at Creighton. Both grieving parents dutifully stood and shook the hands that were offered. Then there was an awkward silence.

"Well, I'll leave you to discuss...your business," Brumback said with a worried glance over to William Hunter. "We'll get back to that case history another time, Bill. No hurry at all. Whenever you..."

Giving it up, Brumback backed out of the room with a tight smile. Negron gave Mois a wide-eyed "how to start?" look. But before he could say anything, Claire Hunter spoke up.

"It must seem strange that we came to work today," she said, almost apologetically. "I'm sure everyone thinks so. But the house is...it's a crime scene, so we can't go in. And we couldn't stand sitting in that hotel room."

Negron gave her an understanding nod. "I think that was a good decision. And we appreciate you seeing us."

Mois took a file out of his briefcase.

"We have a physical description of a person of interest seen in the neighborhood," Mois said as he lay six mug shots down across a small side table. They showed men who all looked to be in their mid-thirties to mid-forties, including Craig Talley. All had medium-to-dark complexions and dark eyes; several had facial hair, one had a shaved head. "Do any of these men look familiar to either of you?"

William Hunter gave his wife a pained glance. But they slowly stood up and, taking one another's hand, cautiously approached the table.

"They all look somewhat alike," William Hunter noted after a moment.

"Yes. Dark hair, cruel eyes," his wife agreed. "But I don't recognize any."

Mois saw that William Hunter was studying the photos with a slightly perplexed expression. "And you, Doctor?"

"No..." he said carefully. "I don't know any of these men. But..."

"Yes?" Negron asked hopefully.

"I'm sorry," he said with certainty. "I don't know them."

Negron took a piece of paper from her briefcase and laid it on the table. "What about this? It's an artist rendering of a description your neighbor gave us."

They both examined the drawing with what seemed equal parts dread and curiosity. The sketch was similar to the photos, although the man depicted had somewhat more swollen cheeks and eyes that were closer together than any of the men in the mug shots. William Hunter looked back and forth between it and the photographs several times.

"Anything?" Mois asked. "Take your time."

Claire Hunter shook her head; her husband looked at the sketch again then reluctantly shook his head.

"What about the name Craig Talley?" Negron asked, trying not to sound too eager. "Does that sound familiar?"

"Not to me," Claire said. "Maybe...someone from Shirlee's family might know him?"

"We're going to find out. I have to stress that we're still early in the investigation," Mois said as he took out another photo. "One last thing, do either of you recall seeing a silver or gray Honda like this in your neighborhood?"

William Hunter glanced at the photo but sighed wearily, "I don't pay much attention to cars."

Claire took the photo but almost immediately shook her head. As Mois picked up the mug shots, the awkward silence again descended.

"When is Tom's funeral?" Negron asked gently.

"Wednesday," Claire replied, sounding grateful at the mention of her son. "They couldn't release the—we've couldn't have Tom back before then."

The detectives said their goodbyes. Both doctors thanked them for coming then slowly resumed their seats. Mois imagined them sitting there for the rest of the day, even into the night. No home to go back to.

"Not very encouraging," Negron sighed as they walked out of the facility. Then, hearing a ping on her phone, she stopped and read the text. "It's Murkowski. He's got Craig Talley's address. He's still in Omaha."

She looked at Mois expectantly. He pondered for a moment—but just a moment. The thought of the shattered couple they had just left renewed his sense of anger.

"Let's do it," he said. "Let's bring that bastard in."

CHAPTER 11

"I'M BEGINNING TO THINK you really got a thing for me, Sergeant Negroni."

Craig Talley—unshaven, dirty jeans, powerfully built but with a rapidly emerging beer belly—sat back in his chair with a self-satisfied grin. He didn't seem the least bit concerned that he was being held in a stark, cement-walled interrogation room. In fact, he gave every indication of enjoying himself.

"That's Sergeant *Negron*, punk," Mois corrected him with a smack on the back of his head. Talley didn't so much as flinch, he just kept his small, jet-black eyes on Teresa. He gave her a long slow leer, lingering on her legs.

"I love a Negroni. One part gin, one part sweet vermouth, one part Campari," Talley said with a smack of his lips. "All parts *delicious*—just like you, Sergeant."

Negron clapped her hands and gave the suspect a big fake grin. "Congrats, Talley—you won! You're officially the two-hundredth asshole to make that joke to me."

Mois walked to the other end of the small table. "You don't seem very curious about why you've been brought in, Talley."

They had picked the suspect up when he came home from his day labor job. His filthy, dilapidated house was in one of Omaha's worst hoods. From the start, Talley had affected a strangely nonchalant attitude. Now, instead of responding to Mois, he stretched back and lifted his feet onto the table; the detective promptly shoved them off.

"Hey, watch the police brutality, dude," Talley whined. "Ain't my fault your partner can't stop obsessing over me. I told her a million times I don't know nothin' about that Blanchard chick."

Mois walked over and, pulling out a chair, took the seat next to Talley. "Big surprise, pal: we didn't bring you in to talk about the Blanchard case."

Talley's eyes nervously narrowed—he'd been caught off guard, finally. Mois could tell the wheels had started turning in his mind.

"Where were you around three p.m. Thursday?" Negron asked in an icy businesslike manner; her abrupt change of tone clearly added to Talley's unease. He warily glanced back and forth between the two detectives.

"Workin', I guess," he shrugged, his brow creased with increasing anxiety.

"Got someone who can verify that?" Mois asked. Talley hesitated a moment, again clearly pondering his situation. Suddenly, a cheesy sham smile spread across his face.

"Now let me see . . . *Hmm*," Talley said with exaggerated effort. "You know what? It's coming to me. Yeah. This is about those murders—the little boy and the cleaning lady, right?"

It didn't throw Negron. She kept her gaze steeled on Talley. He tried to laugh it off but finally smacked the table in exasperation.

"Am I the only guy in Omaha you investigate? What the hell!"

"Where were you?" Mois demanded.

"Pouring concrete, over by the airfield. Worked till seven thirty," Talley stated with absolute conviction. "Boss had to pay us overtime. Wasn't happy about it either. So, guess you two are gonna have to work a little harder on this one."

He stood up and gave a showy stretch. "Either ya'll arrest me or let me go. I know my rights."

Mois pulled him right back down into his chair. "You aren't going anywhere until we talk to your boss. And that could take quite a while. Cell reception sucks down here."

Mois nodded for Negron to join him outside of the interrogation room. As she passed by, Talley made a kissing sound. She seemed ready to whack her folder against the suspect's face, but a warning look from Mois stayed her hand.

Out in the hallway, Negron walked quickly back and forth, releasing a long breath of frustration.

"Seems pretty sure of himself," Mois observed.

"His kind always seem that way, hardly ever really are," she scoffed. "Interesting how he made that jump to the Dundee killings."

Mois nodded as he took out his phone; at the same time, Negron's own cell rang shrilly, echoing up and down the empty hallway.

Mois nodded. "Take it. I'll call Talley's boss."

As Mois punched in numbers, Negron stepped away and glanced at the one-way window into the room where Talley was held. He had turned his chair to face the window and sat grinning with his legs apart, squeezing his crotch. Negron looked away in disgust.

"Yep?" she said into her phone. After listening a bit, her brow furrowed. "Can we come over now?...Great."

She turned back to Mois, who was just getting off his call.

"Bad news. Very bad," he said with a frown. "Talley's boss confirms his alibi. He's not our guy. Sorry, Terry."

Mois was surprised when Negron just gave a cool nod.

"No worries. I'm gonna get Talley someday. I can wait. Until then, I've got *good* news," she said. "You might just have scored with your chat room theory. IT compared chats from Tom Hunter's computer and game console. And they found something."

CHAPTER 12

"THIS PLACE MAKES THE morgue look cheery," Mois whispered to Negron as they entered the strangely darkened digital forensic lab.

"Just go with it," Negron replied. "Tech dudes are a breed apart."

The IT department was downright spooky. The window blinds were all drawn and the overhead lights were off. The only illumination came from the banks of computer monitors, which cast eerie angular shadows over the walls.

Alex Burns, a slim, neatly dressed young technician with a massive brown beard, was typing away on a keyboard. As the two approached, he looked up with a wide smile.

"Welcome to the den of darkness! They let me keep it this way ever since I was diagnosed with SAD—seasonal affective disorder," he said, almost proudly. "I get super depressed when the time changes, so we just keep it dark *all* the time. It totally works!"

Negron shot Mois a "told ya so" glance.

"That's great, Alex," Negron said. "Shows how much the department values you. So, you have some important news on the Hunter case?"

"Oh, *yeah*! Come over here," Alex gestured excitedly as he went to another computer terminal and began punching away at the keyboard. "Tom Hunter logged in some serious gaming hours. And he did a lot of chatting with players online."

Alex pulled up several transcriptions of chat room conversations—mostly written in shortened, slangy text. Mois leaned forward and squinted at the screen; it was so full of emojis it was like trying to read hieroglyphics. "I need my son to translate this! What are they talking about?"

"Standard stuff," Alex said. "Game strategy. Trash-talking opponents. As you probably know, most game software will monitor players' chats. It'll flag things like explicit language, threats, sex talk."

"But what about the locked rooms?" Negron asked. "The private chats? That's what we really need."

Alex gave her a mopey frown. "Unfortunately, that history is wiped clean when the users exit the room."

"Well hell, Alex!" Negron exclaimed in disappointment. "I thought you *had* something."

"So, we're back to square one—again?" Mois sighed.

Raising an eyebrow, Alex glared at one, then the other.

"Um, *excuse* me," he said, thoroughly insulted. "I was just giving background information that you clearly did *not* have. As it happens, I *do* have something for you."

Moving at a much slower pace that seemed intended as payback for the questioning of his abilities, Alex eventually pulled up an entirely new set of transcripts. "It took some work, but I was able to recover quite a few conversations Tom had in private chat rooms."

He looked over his shoulder and, seeing that he now had Mois and Negron's full attention, took a dramatic pause before announcing: "What's more, I tracked down *all* of the user IP addresses and their locations."

An Excel sheet of data suddenly filled the screen with rows and rows of names and physical and digital addresses. As Alex scrolled down, the list seemed never ending.

"Oh lord, that's a lot of names," Negron sighed.

"Just shy of four hundred," Alex confirmed. "*But*, I've been running them down all day. Only about half live in the U.S. And only *one* . . . lives in Omaha."

Mois and Negron looked at each other. Alex spun around in his chair. He gave another showman's pause before delivering his big news.

"*And* not only does he drive a silver Honda CRV . . ." He again expertly raised an eyebrow as he reached across the desk and picked up a print out of a mug shot.

"He's also a registered sex offender."

CHAPTER 13

"IF EVER A SUSPECT checked all the boxes, it's this guy," Negron said as she inhaled her cigarette with relish. Smoking was a vice she allowed herself only in times of celebration. "We got him this time, I know it."

Mois stopped his car across the street from a neglected-looking trailer that sat just five or six feet back from the street. It was a sad sight: the mud-brown paint on the aluminum siding was peeling off in every direction, and bushes and ivy were tangled and wildly overgrown in the front. The place seemed deserted except for a single light shining through a window.

"And, of course, *this* is where the perv lives," Negron noted with scorn. "Perfect."

"Almost too perfect," Mois said carefully. "But for the Hunters' sake, I hope we're onto something."

As the slow spring twilight descended, they sat in Mois's car for a few minutes until a patrol car quietly pulled up behind them. Taking a last satisfied puff,

Negron got out of the car and joined Mois as he approached the officers.

The driver, Officer Nick Johnson, was a small, wiry guy with ultra-smooth skin and a gleaming shaved head. His partner, Officer Erin O'Malley, was his physical opposite: a large woman with a thick thatch of auburn hair and a mass of freckles across her face.

"Good to see you two," Mois said in a hushed voice. "You know what we have here?"

"They filled us in at the station," Johnson said. "You think this guy might be behind the Dundee killings, huh?"

"Do we get to shoot first, question later?" O'Malley asked with a bitter laugh.

Mois frowned. "We're just here to question a person of interest. We don't know much about this guy—he's kept a low profile since he was paroled after a sexual assault conviction. But let's not take chances. He may try to run for it, so, Johnson, you take the back. O'Malley, stay in the car until you hear from one of us."

The officers nodded in agreement. As O'Malley shifted to the driver's seat, Johnson swiftly and noiselessly got out and headed toward the back of the dwelling.

At the front door, Mois pounded twice with so much force the cheap door seemed to buckle. Immediately from inside there was the sound of alarmed movement—shuffling and the rough scraping of a chair across the floor.

"Yes?" said a thin voice from the other side of the door.

"Albert Buckner? Omaha PD. May we come in?"

Silence. Negron instinctively reached for her gun. Mois

rapped again, much louder this time. Finally, the door partially opened to reveal a pale face wearing thick-framed eyeglasses with scuffed lenses.

"Why—what do you want?" the man asked nervously.

Mois pushed the door open further to reveal that the man standing there was hugely overweight, probably morbidly obese. He and Negron exchanged a look—this guy wasn't going to be *running* anywhere.

"What do you want?" Buckner asked again in a high, nervous voice. "You—you need a warrant to come in."

Mois got right in the man's face. "Sure, I can call a judge and get one. It might take fifteen minutes or so. Either way, we're coming in."

Shoulders sagging, Buckner reluctantly stepped back just enough to allow the detectives to squeeze past his enormous stomach.

The inside of the narrow trailer was a mess. Dirty clothes and stained blankets were strewn all over the few pieces of furniture. Several open bags of garbage sat on the floor of the tiny kitchen. A computer monitor sitting on a desk was the only item in the home that wasn't old and falling apart. Negron nodded toward the screen.

"Your parole officer would probably like to know about your Internet surfing," she noted.

"Why? I'm not doing anything wrong," Buckner whined. "I'm *not!*"

Mois looked over the wide-eyed man as he nervously tugged at the drawstring of his grimy sweatpants.

"We're going to need you to come in to the station,"

Mois said calmly. "Answer a few questions about your movements the last few days."

"*Why?* I haven't left the house in—in...well, I don't know, *weeks*, probably," Buckner protested, his agitation rising. "You *can't* send me back to prison. Please. You can't!"

Negron tilted her head at the suspect. "What reason would we have to send you back to prison? What have you done?"

"*Nothing!*" Buckner all but screamed. "I swear! I just can't go back there..."

His face crumpling, the suspect sagged down onto the sofa and began noisily weeping. Negron gave Mois a knowing nod—"guilt" was written all over this guy.

"Bring O'Malley in," Mois said. "I'm going to have a look around."

Taking out his flashlight, Mois went down a hallway. He noted a disheveled bedroom, then another door leading out back.

The yard was so chaotically filthy it made the inside of the house look pristine. Piles of junk littered the area, including a cracked and repulsively stained old toilet. Darting his light to the left, Mois saw that Johnson was at work examining a large object nearly buried under an overgrown bush.

"Car tarp," the officer said as he untied a loose rope. Mois bent down and together they pulled the cloth back to reveal the front of the vehicle.

"Right on the money," Mois said excitedly. "Silver Honda CRV!"

He then scanned his flashlight further down.

Both front tires were flat and sunken into the ground. The entire underside of the chassis was deeply, corrosively rusted.

Mois sighed. "And it probably hasn't been driven in at least five years."

The back door opened and Negron stepped out. At the sight of the car, a pumped-up grin spread across her face. "O'Malley is with Buckner. We got our man, gents!"

Negron dug into her jacket pocket and pulled out her cigarettes. But she paused when she saw the deflated expressions on Mois and Johnson's faces. She gave them a miffed, questioning stare.

"Sergeant Negron," Mois said with a rueful smile. "I think you might have smoked too soon..."

CHAPTER 14

TWO PEOPLE WERE DEAD.

Brutally murdered. No stealth was involved. Nor were there any signs of advance planning. As if the killer hadn't cared whether he was caught or not.

And yet somehow Detective Derek Mois still was no closer to a suspect or a motive than he was six days earlier when Tom Hunter and Shirlee Sherman were slain.

Mois knew that beating himself up wasn't going to change anything. But it was tough not to feel frustration and guilt, especially standing at Tom's burial service. He'd attended Shirlee Sherman's funeral the day before; the questioning look on her daughter Kelly's face lingered in his mind. He'd had no answers for her.

At least yesterday had been sunny and warm. Today was cloudy and a constant chilly breeze made the occasion that much grimmer. Still, it was a well-attended service, with a crowd of onlookers and a TV camera van hovering at the edge of the lush and leafy cemetery. Standing among the mourners, Mois looked on as the Hunters clutched each other next to their son's grave. Their expressions were pure anguish. Two white-faced young men in dark, ill-fitting suits stood at their sides. Mois assumed they were the older sons.

As the service ended, people began approaching the Hunters to offer condolences. Mois saw that one of the first to reach them was the older man he'd met in Hunter's lab, the fellow doctor with the warm smile. He racked his brain for the name. Then, it came to him: Roger Brumback.

A few moments later, Brumback and his small, energetic-looking wife, Mary, approached Mois. After introductions were made, Mois noted that each had the same searching looks on their faces that he'd gotten from Kelly Wedgewood.

"How are the Hunters holding up?" Mois asked with real concern.

Brumback shook his head. "They're destroyed. I thought having the older boys back from school would help, but the kids are just as devastated."

He continued giving Mois that expectant look.

"I wish I had some news for them," the detective said. "We've had some leads, but none have panned out. Though, of course, the investigation continues."

Brumback frowned. "It's the *reason* I keep coming back to. Why would anyone do this to that wonderful little boy and that sweet woman? *Why?*"

Again, Mois had nothing.

"What about that artist's drawing?" Mary Brumback asked hopefully. "The one they showed on TV the other day? The man with the awful little eyes."

Mois shook his head regretfully. "Several people in the Hunters' neighborhood confirmed seeing someone matching the likeness. But, no, it hasn't led to any arrests. Not yet, anyway."

The Brumbacks nodded in disappointment, then shook Mois's hand goodbye. The persistent breeze suddenly turned into a full gust, prompting the Hunters to finally move slowly away from the gravesite.

As Claire Hunter introduced her sons to some mourners, Mois respectfully approached William Hunter.

"Detective Mois," the doctor said. "Nice of you to attend."

"Of course," Mois said. "And Sergeant Negron asked me to give you her regards. She was put on—she had to attend to some matters relating to another investigation."

William Hunter looked directly in Mois's eye. "Has she been taken off my son's case?"

"No—well, not taken off," Mois said hesitantly. "But a little girl went missing yesterday and—"

"Yes, I read about it. I understand," Hunter said sadly. He looked across the cemetery. The onlookers were dispersing and the attendees were trudging back to their cars. The sole camera van was pulling out of the parking lot.

"The reporters and TV trucks have left our neighborhood," Dr. Hunter noted. "I guess the story is old news already..."

Mois reached out and took the doctor's hand. "It isn't to me, Doctor. I'm sorry I don't have more developments to share. But I'm determined to find your son's killer. I can't tell you how long it may take, but I won't stop looking."

Hunter nodded slowly with a small smile of thanks.

"I believe *you* won't give up, Detective Mois," the doctor said. "I just wish I could say the same about myself..."

CHAPTER 15

AS THE SERVICE ENDED, the cool wind picked up sharply, causing suit jackets to flap open and scarves to dart around like sparrows. The wind seemed intent on clearing the cemetery out as quickly as possible. The lingering mourners hurried toward their cars, eager to escape the elements as well as the sadness of the occasion.

Chilled, the small man zipped his windbreaker up all the way to his jowly neck. He should have worn something heavier, but it was nearly April and no one had expected this cold spell. He also shouldn't have worn a red jacket—the bright, cheery color had attracted more than a few disapproving glares. But he had just squinted back at them with his small black eyes, daring anyone to say a word. Daring anyone to question his presence there.

Daring anyone to recognize him.

He looked across the cemetery and watched as the Hunters carefully got into a shining black Lincoln Town Car. One of the two tall boys climbed into the back with his parents; the other went to sit in the front passenger seat. The funeral procession then slowly wound its way out of the parking lot, moving past what remained of the mourners. The Town Car drove right by the man, not more than ten feet away, the dark tinted windows shielding the faces and the grief inside. As it drove off, the man wondered if anyone in the vehicle had noticed him standing on the side of the road.

If so, he hoped they had seen his wide, satisfied smile.

PART TWO

CHAPTER 16

May 9, 2013
Terre Haute, Indiana

NO ONE SEES ME. I'm standing here wearing less fabric than you'd find on a spool of thread and no one *sees* me.

Mia Vaughn had the same thought night after night while dancing at the Sixth Avenue gentlemen's club. "Dancing." That was a joke. She wriggled, she swayed, she lifted her legs, she shook her shoulders. That wasn't dancing. Technically, it wasn't even stripping. She came out onto the stage wearing only her tiny thong which, legally, couldn't come off. The men leered at her, joked with her, tried to grope her. But they never saw her.

Mia spun her bouncy blond hair around and glanced at the clock above the bar. Just two minutes left of her set. And she'd been tipped a grand total of eighteen dollars. She was furious at herself for spending the money she had this afternoon at the tanning booth. What a waste! She had hoped to clear at least seventy-five dollars this night so she could take her son to the doctor. He'd had a persistent cough that she kept telling herself would go away. Now, unless the crowd really picked up, she'd have to take him to the free clinic first thing in the morning. The wait would be endless. And she had a lunch shift at her day job.

One more minute to go, not a lifted dollar in sight. Mia then saw the club's front door open and, miraculously, her most reliable regular came in—second night in a row! Mia didn't know his name but thought of him as "Red Windbreaker Guy" or just "Red." The tatty old jacket was all she'd ever seen the squat, somewhat chubby man wear, even when it was freezing. Some kind of security blanket quirk, she guessed. He could certainly afford a new coat; he always tipped her—and her alone—generously.

As he ordered a drink, Mia tried to catch his eye, but the music abruptly changed and the next girl, Jessi, sauntered out. Mia reluctantly started toward the back of the stage but, on a whim, decided to hop off the platform. She wanted to approach Red at the bar before one of the other girls, even though she usually liked to put on her gauzy wrap before mingling.

"Hey! You just missed my set!"

He slowly turned around and gave Mia an intent lingering smile. Red had a slightly pear-shaped head; his chubby cheeks seemed to unfortunately emphasize that his eyes were just a little too close together. Mia always tried to look past Red's obvious weirdo vibe. She told herself that even if there was something off in those very small, very dark eyes, at least *he* saw her.

"My loss," he said in his oddly gruff voice. "But I can still tip ya, right?"

He reached into his jacket pocket and pulled out a small orange plastic bottle, clearly some kind medication. He handed it to her.

"What—what's this?" Mia asked in disappointed confusion. Did he think she was a speed freak or something?

"It's for your son."

Mia just stared at him blankly.

"You told me about his cough," he said. "That's a low-level antibiotic. Twice a day and that cough will be gone."

Mia was flabbergasted. "*What?* Oh, my god! That is *so* nice of you!"

Red just stood there, smiling away, not taking his eyes off her. Mia then glanced down at the medication label. "But—I mean, Jake's only five. Are you sure this, I mean, is it all right for kids?"

Red turned the label around. "Call that eight-hundred number. It's staffed twenty-four-seven. Tell them the symptoms and they'll tell you that this is what Jake needs."

"I can't believe you did this for me!" Mia said, almost tearfully. Red not only saw her, but he'd *listened* to her when she'd expressed concern about her son. "How did you get them?"

He shrugged casually, obviously trying for bravado. "I get things done. I do the things most people don't have the nerve to do."

Mia felt her smile fall a bit, but she gave a laugh and

said kiddingly, "Oh wow, sounds like you're in the Mafia or something!"

Red just kept smiling and staring with those intent little eyes.

"Oh, hell," Mia sighed. "I don't care. You've helped me more than anyone has, like, *ever*. I totally owe you."

She impulsively leaned forward and gave Red a quick, tight hug. As she pulled away, he reached out and took her hand. He held it, clearly not wanting to let go. She was surprised; he'd never even tried to touch her before.

"Go out with me," he said. It wasn't exactly a question, a little more like a demand.

"Oh, that is so nice of you! But I can't," Mia said with what she hoped sounded like sincere regret. "We're not allowed to go out with clients. It's the rules. My boss, JJ, would have a fit. He's such a dick."

Red didn't get angry or look disappointed. But he did stop smiling.

"Think about it," he said as he squeezed her hand harder. "I'm going out of town this weekend. Some big business to attend to. Maybe I'll check back in a few days."

Mia wavered. He wasn't pressuring her—not really. And he seemed genuinely interested in her. Yes, he was a little sketchy and he wasn't attractive *at all* and what the hell was with that jacket? But then again, he'd been so incredibly kind to her. And not just tonight.

She smiled warmly at him. "Okay. Maybe check back."

After all, she asked herself, what real harm could there be?

CHAPTER 17

FROM WHAT HE COULD tell, Omaha hadn't changed one bit since the murders. Or, at least this upscale part of town looked exactly the same as he remembered from his frequent drive-bys. Nice homes, nice cars, nice people. People with successful careers. Money. Respect. And the sense of entitlement that came with all that. You could see it on every one of their smug, smiling faces. Even the children.

After parking the car, he rolled down his window and felt the warm early-morning breeze. It had been a long drive from Terre Haute and he was tired. He needed sleep but business came first. He double-checked his notes and confirmed that he was across from the correct address—a well-maintained, two-story beige house. But still, he hesitated getting out of the car. The timing—the feeling—had to be just right.

There was no hurry.

He pulled off his windbreaker and reached under the

seat for his flask. He took a large swig, then another. As he relaxed, his thoughts drifted back over the years—back two years, then five years and then ten. He realized he'd been heading toward this particular destination for a long time. It might take him a while—years sometimes—but, just as he'd told his girlfriend Mia, he was a guy who got things done.

He decisively reached into his duffel bag and pulled out a sleek black handgun.

When he rang the doorbell, he heard the elegant chimes echo musically throughout the house. Then he heard overlapping voices inside—a man and a woman's. A back-and-forth, exasperated-sounding argument about who would answer the door. He rang the bell again, harder this time, making the chimes sound a bit more insistent in their lilting echo. Finally, he heard a somewhat annoyed, "Honey, *I* will get it!" and a few seconds later the door opened.

The man was in his mid-sixties, balding, fit though just a little stooped in his posture. He was wearing a faded Huskers T-shirt and old cargo shorts, clearly his weekend working clothes. He had a warm smile.

"Hi there, sorry for the wait. Moving day—always the worst!" he said with a slightly put-upon sigh. "You're here to get the piano? You're a little early, but that's okay."

He glanced out past the man standing on his front porch. "Where's your truck?"

He then did a double-take. He leaned forward slightly to look a little closer at the squat dark man with the strange eyes. "Hey. I think—"

"Hello, Doctor."

A confused silence.

"Wait—are—"

Pulling out his gun, the man aimed and shot Roger Brumback directly in the center of his chest.

CHAPTER 18

THE SHARP BANG ECHOED throughout the house—just as that infernal doorbell had. Good lord, wasn't this morning chaotic *enough* without all this noise?

Mary Brumback looked away from her computer monitor in irritation.

"What's wrong, Mom?"

The harried woman turned back to her Skype chat. "Oh, sweetie, the piano movers are here and I'm sure your father is trying to tell them what to do and just getting in their way. I heard a loud bang, like they've already *dropped* it!"

Mary's daughter, Audrey, hoped the dim camera optics hid her amused smile. She tipped her head a little to let her long bangs fall forward. Oh, was she ever glad she was safely away from this scene in her San Francisco apartment. As much as she loved her parents—and knew they loved each other—the dynamics of any Brumback family project usually involved a fair amount of irritated bickering.

"I'll let you go then, Mom," Audrey said with a waved kiss to the camera. "It sucks that you're spending Mother's Day moving. Make Dad take you out for a nice dinner—an *expensive* one!"

Mary smiled distractedly back at her daughter. "Oh, who knows when we'll be finished with all this. But I'll be fine—as long as I can have my glass of chardonnay at the end of it all. I love you, sweetie—thanks so much for calling!"

After more mimed kisses, the women logged off. With a pained sigh, Mary stood up, stretched, and went into the nearby guest bathroom. Looking in the mirror, she said out loud, "My *hair*!" Even though she wore her frosted hair short, it seemed to be sticking out in every direction this morning. She thought she must have looked like a madwoman to her daughter. She certainly didn't want the movers to see her like this. Picking up a comb, she brushed and fussed until it was at least tamped down. In the background, she overheard Roger moving about in the kitchen.

Entering the bedroom again, she bent to pick up another flattened moving box and started opening it up.

"Roger?" she called out. "Audrey sends her love. What on *earth* was going on out there?"

At first Mary heard only silence but then the squeak of the hallway floorboards as someone crossed them.

"Roger?"

The house went silent again. Her patience already sorely tested, Mary dropped the box and marched out into the kitchen. Though the floor was nearly covered with boxes, the table, sink, and counters were all spotless. But as she walked through the room, Mary saw that her walnut butcher-block knife set had been taken out of the open box she had just put it in *not twenty minutes ago*! It was sitting on the counter, and two of the knives were missing. Surely Roger wasn't using her good cooking knives to cut twine or packing tape? Or was he letting the piano movers use them?

She strode into the living room. "Roger!"

No one was there. In fact, the piano was still sitting in its usual place. Then *what* had caused that racket, Mary wondered. She stepped up to the bay window and looked outside. There was no moving truck in front. The street was empty except for a silver SUV parked in front of the Coopers'.

"Roger!" she shouted this time. *Where* was that man? Had he gone to the garage?

Mary entered the foyer and started toward the front door.

And then she saw Roger sprawled flat on his back.

In her shock, the first thought that crossed Mary's mind was that her husband had had a massive heart attack.

But that didn't explain the gaping wound in the dead center of his chest, as if the Huskers logo on his T-shirt had been used as a bullseye.

Mary gave a strangled scream. The world seemed to turn upside down and she involuntarily staggered backward, away from the horrifying sight.

She backed up right into someone's arms—which was startling yet somehow comforting, too. One arm came around her chest, as if to prevent her from collapsing. But the other arm flew through the air in front of her—first up, then down. The hallway light bounced off the side of the knife the person was holding. One of the sharp knives with the distinctive dark walnut handles.

Long, horrible moments later, Mary Brumback slid to the floor a few feet away from her husband.

Her good cooking knife was sticking out of her throat.

CHAPTER 19

HOW COULD ANYTHING BE wrong on beautiful, sunny, calm Sunday morning like this—Mother's Day yet, for Christ's sake? The day was just too perfect for any kind of emergency. Derek Mois decided whatever it was could wait another ten minutes while he finished his five-mile jog.

Since turning forty—and finding gray hairs sprouting up through the tattoos on his forearms—Mois had made it a personal goal to run three times a week. And he'd stuck to it religiously. If he stopped to answer his buzzing cell, he wouldn't finish this run and he'd blow his perfect record. Keeping commitments was important to the detective, even ones he'd only made to himself.

He did the last mile and a half in ninety seconds under his usual time. Not bad for an old guy, he thought. He entered the house through the back door and went into the kitchen for some water. Danny was at the table, tapping away on his laptop.

"Dad, what took you so long? We're going to be late!" his son cried as he looked up with concern. "There's going to be a *huge* line at the theater!"

Mois couldn't believe how much Danny had grown in the past year or so. He was already an inch taller than his father, and didn't look to be slowing down any time soon. Most unnerving of all to Mois was the faint but definite goatee Danny was growing. Gone were the gawky, skinny frame, the crooked teeth, and the horribly uncool eyeglasses. That boy no longer existed. The image caused Mois's mind to turn to another long-gone adolescent: Tom Hunter, the kid who never got to outgrow his awkwardness. Five years ago. The case still unsolved, despite the assurances Mois had given Tom's father. *So much for delivering on my commitments*, the detective thought bitterly.

"*Dad!*"

Danny's voice snapped Mois out of his dark thoughts. He took a long, slow drink of water, teasing out the delay. Danny's eyes grew wide at his father's seeming indifference to his worry. Finally, Mois put the glass down and casually said, "Dude, I'm all over this."

"What do you mean?" Danny asked with suspicion.

Mois broke into a big smile. "I already bought the movie tickets online, pal. Paid extra for the reserved seating section."

"*Really?*" Danny brightened. "You got one for Charlie too, right?"

"Charlie, too."

They were going to see the latest superhero movie—try

as he might, Mois could never tell one from another—at Omaha's newest stadium seating theatre. Reclining leather seats, eardrum-shattering Dolby sound, drive-in-sized movie screens. Since Mois's wife had taken her own mom out for a Mother's Day Champagne breakfast, the boys had the morning to themselves. Mois had felt a pang of guilt at how excited—and surprised—Danny had been when he'd suggested they see the film. It made him realize how long it had been since they'd spent time together.

"I'm going to jump in the shower. Be ready in five minutes, pal," Mois said as he bounded out of the kitchen.

"Hurry, I don't want to miss the trailers!" Danny called after him. "And don't forget you promised an extra-extra-large popcorn!"

As Mois took the stairs two at a time, his cell phone buzzed again. He'd forgotten to check his voice mail. He pulled the phone out of his running shorts and saw a text from Teresa Negron:

Answer phone! DOUBLE homicide!!!

Mois slumped against the wall in disbelief. There hadn't been a killing in the Omaha metro area since January. Why *today*?

"Four minutes, Dad!" Danny yelled.

As he turned to go back down the stairs, Mois could literally feel his heart break. At this moment, a double murder—however horrible the scene—sounded a lot easier to face than giving his son this news.

Commitments, Mois said to himself. *Yeah, I'm all over them...*

CHAPTER 20

"SO, I SEE THAT the front door is open an inch or two. And I lean forward just a little, and that's when I see it. A gun clip layin' right there on the floor! A *gun clip*—in a house like this!"

The large middle-aged man with a beet-red face gestured dramatically as he related his story to Negron and another officer. He was wearing a black T-shirt that said JASON PETERSON, THE PIANO MAN. As Mois approached the front of the residence, he saw that a truck with the same printing on its side was sitting in the driveway. Two patrol cars were parked at haphazard angles in the street, and a flashing ambulance sat between them.

"So, I push on the door, but it wouldn't budge no more—like something's blockin' it," Peterson continued, raising his voice. "That's when I start thinkin' I better call the cops, and *pronto*!"

Negron looked up and saw Mois coming up the drive. She put her hand on the other officer's forearm then hurried over toward Mois. She noted the set jaw that indicated his mood was a dark one. After five and a half years of working together, she knew his every expression.

"Why so grim?" Negron asked. "You haven't even seen what's inside yet."

"The timing of this is *not* optimal," Mois all but snarled.

"Wow, pardner," Negron said incredulously. "You mean there's a *good* time for a double murder?"

Mois frowned and shook his head, abashed.

"No, of course not," Mois said apologetically. "Scratch that comment from the record. It's just I had plans with Danny, and I'm probably going to have to buy him a car to get him to speak to me again."

Negron gave his shoulder an understanding squeeze. "I'm pretty sure Danny's going to forgive you when he hears the details on this one. Come on, we gotta go through the back. One of the bodies is blocking the front door."

Mois followed after Negron as she quickly went up the drive to a side door that lead into the kitchen. As they entered, Mois noted the array of differently sized moving boxes stacked around the otherwise tidy room.

"Fill me in. What do we have?" Mois asked.

Negron stopped Mois in his tracks before he could advance any further.

"I don't know how to tell you this," she said, a bit breathlessly. "We have a husband and wife. Retired doctor. He was shot once in the chest and stabbed multiple times. But the thing is—"

"Stabbed first, then shot?" Mois asked impatiently.

"I don't know! Just *listen* to me, Mois!" Negron nearly screamed. "Because this is *major*. You're not going to believe it. Both victims have, well...ah hell, just come and see for yourself."

Negron pulled Mois toward a small sitting room off of the front foyer. Two ashen-faced patrolman—rookies, Mois assumed, from their obvious youth and shocked expressions—were standing guard. On the floor, a silver-haired woman in her sixties was lying on her side. Blood was everywhere—all over her clothes, all over the floor, all over the walls. Mois took in the grisly sight as stoically as he could, then did a double-take.

A long kitchen knife was sticking up out of the side of the woman's throat.

Mois shot Negron an astonished look. Wide-eyed, she gestured to his right toward the front door. Mois looked over and saw a man in his sixties lying flat on his back. A horrific chest wound ringed with darkening blood initially demanded Mois's attention—until he saw another knife sticking out of the side of the man's throat.

Mois turned to Negron—they just gaped at each other for a beat.

"He's back," she said in a stunned whisper. "The bastard has struck again!"

His mind reeling, Mois quickly paced from one body to the other. He immediately saw that woman had not been shot, she'd only been stabbed—but many times, countless times. Defensive wounds laced her arms and hands— she'd put up a fight.

"Okay, just hold on now," Mois said, trying for calm as he went over to take a closer look at the man's body. "This could be a copycat."

"Not a chance!" Negron protested. "The MO is too specific!"

"But the Hunter crime scene details are well known. The knives left in the throats made headlines," Mois cautioned. "For Christ's sake, they even used it on a *Law & Order* episode. And don't forget, no gun was used in the killings at the Hunters' house."

"And don't *you* forget that it was never revealed that the knives were taken from the Hunters' kitchen block set," Negron said pointedly. "Just take a guess where these knives came from."

In continuing disbelief, Mois stepped past one of the frozen patrolmen and glanced into the kitchen. There it was: an expensive-looking dark-wood knife set sitting in the middle of the counter. Two knives were missing.

"You are way ahead of me, Negron," Mois acknowledged as he looked over the front of the house. "Who are these people, anyway?"

The sergeant looked at her notes. "Dr. Roger Brumback. And his wife, Mary."

Mois worked a hand over his chin, trying to process this confounding scene. He looked around the house again, finally zeroing in on the sitting room. After a beat, he strode quickly across the room and picked something up from a small side table.

"Wait—Roger *Brumback*? We *met* him!" Mois exclaimed. "We met him in Dr. Hunter's office."

Mois turned around and held up a large coffee mug for Negron to see. "This is it—this is the link!"

On the side of the hefty ceramic cup was a sky-blue logo: CREIGHTON UNIVERSITY SCHOOL OF MEDICINE.

CHAPTER 21

"**TWO—*POSSIBLY* THREE—MURDERS** committed in 2008. Then, in 2013, two more murders. Five killings, five years apart."

Confused murmuring rippled across the room.

"The math doesn't make sense to us now, but it will eventually—it *has* to."

Mois let his words sink in to the multiagency task force he was addressing. It was a sizeable group—the largest Mois had ever headed up. About fifteen people were crammed into the Omaha PD's biggest conference room. Rows of long tables had been set up classroom style facing the speaker podium where Mois stood with Negron at his side. Laptops were open, pencils were held at the ready, all eyes were wide. The energy in the room was crackling—it was an exciting case. Mois could see and feel the intense dedication pouring out of every officer and technician that sat in front of him.

Mois gave a nod to Alex Burns, who sat on his left with

a laptop perched on a crossed knee. Alex's once massive beard was a now thing of the past, an apparent casualty of his having been made head of the IT department; he now worked a much more buttoned-down look. He clicked a few keys and the white screen behind Mois lit up. A slow dissolve revealed smiling photographs of Tom Hunter and Shirlee Sherman on the left side of the page, Joy Blanchard appeared in the middle, and then Roger and Mary Brumback came into view on the right.

"Four of the five victims were stabbed in the neck and the knives left there," Mois said as he used a pointer to indicate Tom, Shirlee, and the Brumbacks. "The fifth— Joy Blanchard—had two knives stuck into her *head*. We remain unsure if this killing is related. There are differences in the attack. Foremost, the stabbings seem random, not focused on the throat. And, Ms. Blanchard was probably already dead when the knives entered her skull. In the other cases, the killer seemed to be searching for the carotid arteries and jugular veins. The killer knew what he—or she—was doing. It's the kind of thing a doctor or medical student would know how to do."

Mois nodded for the next slide. A new photograph flashed on the screen: William Hunter standing with Roger Brumback, their arms slung over one another's shoulders at some kind of professional function. Big, happy smiles from both men.

"Two doctors from the pathology department at the Creighton School of Medicine. Colleagues who are also linked by these murders. Why?"

With a wave of his hand, Mois signaled two officers standing at the doorway to enter. They wheeled in a cart containing stacks of large banker's boxes labeled CREIGHTON UNIVERSITY PERSONNEL. The men began lining the boxes up on a table directly in front of the podium.

"We've requisitioned all of the university's personnel files from the mid-eighties to present day," Mois said. "Yeah, there's a lot of them—and we have more documents that exist in digital form only. But we need to comb through *every* file and read *every* single page—from staff evaluations to recommendation letters to disciplinary actions. We need to find someone with a grudge against Dr. William Hunter *and* Dr. Roger Brumback."

Another murmur rippled through the assembled task force. The scale of the project seemed immense, even with the considerable manpower on hand.

Mois gave his audience a sympathetic smile. "This is going to be tedious, it's going to be boring, it's going to be extremely time-consuming. This isn't the glamour part of police work. But it's absolutely essential."

He paused for a moment then nodded back at Alex. The screen went back to the original image of the five victims.

"Your efforts will help lead us to this killer," Mois said. "He's *somewhere* in one of these boxes. So, let's dig in. Let's find the justice that these five people deserve."

CHAPTER 22

LIFE AND DEATH—AND every possible issue in between, from major to minor to downright petty.

That's all Mois could think after a full day of plowing through the Creighton files. Pay raises, pay disputes, maternity leave, insubordination, promotions, demotions— the different types of paperwork that had to be processed were endless. Mois stared at the document in front of him: an employee complaint to HR stating that she was lactose intolerant and unable to eat the ice cream cake that had been served at an office birthday party. *If she's not psycho enough to hold a murderous grudge, I don't know who is,* Mois thought.

He looked up tiredly and saw through the windows that ran the length of the room that night had fallen without his even noticing. After over eight hours of working, the team was only about a third of the way through the file boxes that lined the front table. Most of the staff had left for the day.

Mois glanced over at Negron, who was seated next to him and examining a sheaf of papers. She looked bleary-eyed but intent.

"Whaddaya got?" he asked.

"An expense report from an obstetrician," Negron said. "He tried to pass off a $242.00 bar charge as a client meeting. Wouldn't his clients be *pregnant* women? And he was getting them *drunk*?"

"Sounds like he was trying to engage in some 'fertility research' to me," Mois laughed. "Let's shut down for the night. I'm gonna be seeing payroll analysis reports in my sleep."

With a sigh, he checked how many documents there were left in the May 2001 file that was open in front of him. Since there were only five or six remaining, he forced himself to do a quick scan. After going through several, he read the front of a two-page letter. He then turned the page.

What he saw made him stand up from his chair.

"Alex!" he said to the IT wizard who was wearily scrolling through some of Creighton's digital files. "Run a PD check on a guy named Anthony Garcia."

Alex gave a limp mock salute and, showily yawning, launched a search.

"Whadda *you* got?" Negron asked, curious at Mois's apparent excitement.

Mois handed her the paper. "In 2001, a resident named Anthony Garcia was fired. Here's his termination letter."

Negron took it and quickly skimmed the letter aloud:

"'*Dr. Garcia is very passive/aggressive...He has repeatedly shown a marked lack of initiative and interest...Dr. Garcia takes no responsibility for his cases...His knowledge is very poor.'* Geez, not exactly Employee of the Month material."

"Turn the page. Look who signed it."

Negron did a startled double-take. "Dr. Roger Brumback—*and* Dr. William Hunter!"

Mois took the letter back and began pacing as he ran over the implications. "This is pretty damning stuff, could be basis for a grudge. But the date...This was written so long ago—*seven* years before the Hunter-Sherman murders. Why wait so long if the killings were payback for getting fired?"

Just then Alex gave a low grunt.

"Found only one Anthony Garcia, and he's a real piece of work," he said. "Multiple DUIs. Nuisance calls to the police. Disturbance complaints from his neighbors."

"Anything violent?" Mois asked.

"Doesn't look like it. But he's a definite 'sooner or later' case, if ya ask me," Alex replied with another yawn.

"Keep digging," Mois said as he checked his watch. "I wonder if it's too late to call Dr. Hunter about this guy?"

"Hold on, let's check something else," Negron said as she quickly tapped into her laptop. "Alex, see if there's a Creighton employee photo for Garcia. If not, do a DMV check on that name."

Now aware that something important might be going down, Alex shook his head to fully wake himself and grabbed one of the back-up drives that the university had provided. He entered a search for Anthony Garcia. A dizzying row of results came up; Alex narrowed the field to "jpeg" and after a few seconds a color head shot popped up.

"Bingo!" Alex exclaimed. "Damn, that was fast—even by my standards. Looks like this is the photo used for his staff badge."

Mois looked over at the monitor and slapped the table top.

"*Bingo* is an understatement!" he said excitedly. "Negron, I'm thinkin' this guy looks just like—"

"The original artist's sketch," Negron said as she turned her laptop around to display the five-year-old drawing of a dark-haired, dark-eyed suspect.

It was a nearly exact rendering of the man who stared back from the Creighton University School of Medicine ID badge—right down to the small, beady, cruel eyes.

CHAPTER 23

"IT'S THE SAME KILLER, isn't it?"

Dr. Hunter asked the question with eyes full of both hope and fear.

Mois hadn't even crossed the threshold of the doctor's office door before Hunter spoke. Of course, it would already have occurred to him, Mois realized. That the person who killed his son might also have killed his colleague. Hunter must have spent the past five years with Tom's murder always at the forefront of his mind. Every crime reported in every news story was a possible link to the person responsible for his child's death. But Mois was sure Hunter had never before imagined that another crime would touch him so closely, so horribly.

"It's a definite possibility," Mois said in a measured tone as he came into the room. The office was brightly lit, unlike the last time he'd been there; sunshine streamed in from an east-facing window. The sunniness made Mois feel slightly uneasy, as though his presence brought in a dark reminder of past pain.

"There are some strong similarities in the killings of your son, Shirlee Sherman, and the Brumbacks," Mois confirmed. "And we're looking at a potential suspect. Do you remember a doctor here named Anthony Garcia?"

Hunter gave a start and sat forward. "Yes, sure. He was a resident. But we let him go from our program, years ago—at least eight or nine. In fact—"

With a businesslike pivot, Hunter picked up his glasses from the desk and turned to his computer keyboard. He began methodically searching his files. "Let's see...Yes, Anthony Garcia. Fired in 2001 for trying to sabotage a colleague's medical exam. Oh lord, that was a mess...I remember his attitude was very poor. He had a history of treating staff members with rudeness and aggression."

He turned to look questioningly back at Mois.

"Garcia was a terrible employee but...why would you think he's responsible for the—the killings?" Hunter asked, cautiously—as though he wasn't sure he was fully prepared for the answer.

"It's possible that Garcia might hold some sort of grudge against you. But it's *just* a possibility," Mois emphasized. "Do you remember anything about this guy that might suggest he'd be capable of violence?"

Closing his eyes, Hunter rubbed his forehead for a moment; this out-of-the-blue possibility had clearly shaken him. But after a moment, he briskly turned back to his computer and flicked through more files.

"We've had so many residents since then. Let me just go through his history," Hunter said while reading from a document onscreen. "Okay, yes, there was another incident: Garcia mishandled an autopsy case, the body of an obese woman. He left her in the refrigerated chamber lying *facedown*. The poor woman's body became horribly disfigured—the family was unable to have an open-casket funeral. An inexcusable mistake. That's something a first-*day* medical student would know not to do!"

Mois nodded sympathetically, in a way he hoped would hide the frustration he was feeling. So far, it was a stretch to connect a lousy employee to a vicious murderer.

"I see. It sounds like—well—like these are all examples of poor performance or judgment, but they don't really suggest a violent or vengeful person."

Hunter shrugged helplessly. "I just don't know. But he could certainly hold a grudge. He took everything very personally. Except his duties. He once got into a screaming match with Chandra—Dr. Chandra Bewtra. He refused to apologize and after that would never directly address her. It was very childish."

"Did he ever threaten that doctor or anyone else?" Mois asked intently. "Has he ever come back here?"

The doctor was beginning to seem overwhelmed by trying to recall his past associations with Garcia.

"Ah, I don't know of any threats. I'm sorry. And I don't know why he would ever have come back here. No one liked him," Hunter said as he continued clicking through files, a little desperately now. "Oh, there was this: Garcia failed his residency. Which, of course, we had to report."

"What does that mean?" Mois asked, his interest piqued.

Hunter again rubbed his forehead. Mois noticed that his hands were shaking, and feared the questions and the disturbing possibilities they were raising were torture to the doctor.

"In order to issue a medical license," Hunter said carefully, as though trying to connect the dots he was presenting. "The state board has to verify a doctor's training. It's routine. But Garcia failed his, miserably."

Hunter continued clicking through files—more quickly and with growing frustration.

"I know I have some correspondence here. I'm sure I kept it," the doctor said as he squinted over an email chain. "Here! Garcia protested the result of his test…Then Dr. Brumback responded to a board inquiry in September of 2007 and then I—"

The doctor froze. He then slowly turned to Mois with an ashen face.

"I responded to another inquiry in February of 2008."

The meaning behind that date became instantly clear to both men.

"The month before Tom was killed," Mois said.

"Do you think that's *it*?" Hunter gasped, looking flabbergasted. "Garcia blames *us* for keeping him from being a doctor?"

Mois raised his hands, trying to calm the now thoroughly shaken man across the desk from him. "*Maybe*. But this does suggest a motive—a motive a very sick individual might act upon."

Hunter collapsed forward, his hands covering his face as sobs racked his body. Mois realized he had brought much more into this room than a dark reminder of the past; he'd brought in a dark present, a new living hell.

"Dear God," Hunter cried, choked with reborn grief. "Why didn't the bastard just kill *me*?"

CHAPTER 24

"OKAY—ADMITTEDLY, I DID make the mistake of saying this once before," Negron excitedly said to Mois as he entered the task force room. "*But*, this Garcia guy checks *all* the boxes!"

The conference room was buzzing with staff. About twelve personnel were working the phones, doing online searches, or continuing to plow through the Creighton files—in some cases, all three simultaneously. Mois noted that a large map of the Midwest had been tacked up on the back wall. He gave Negron a nod as he took his seat at the front table.

"Actually, I don't think you're jumping the gun this time, Terry," Mois said as he booted up his laptop. "Looks very much like Garcia is our guy."

As he started silently typing up his notes, Negron gave him a puzzled look.

"Wow, keep your excitement level in check," she said sarcastically. "Remember your nonexistent heart condition."

Mois kept typing away without looking up. "I just came back from seeing Hunter. The disciplinary actions he took against Garcia absolutely suggest that this guy holds him and Brumback responsible for torpedoing his career."

"That's great!" Negron exclaimed. "I mean—*isn't* it?"

With a long sigh, Mois indicated for Negron to take a seat next to him.

"It is great—for us. We finally have our motive. But...you gotta see that it's devastating for Hunter. His son, housekeeper, close colleague, and the colleague's wife all may have been murdered because of *his* interactions with a disgruntled employee."

Negron frowned thoughtfully as she took in how shattering this revelation must have been for the doctor.

"But—he can't blame himself," she protested. "Whatever actions he took against Garcia were *required* of him— he was doing his job! Just like we are."

"You know that, *I* know it," Mois agreed. "But I'm not sure Dr. Hunter ever will."

Just then, Alex came bounding over clutching a printout.

"Got new intel on Garcia from DMV!" he said, clearly stoked. "In 2001, he registered a vehicle: silver Honda CRV! At this point, I'm thinking case *closed*! Am I right, people?"

He held his palm up for a high-five, but the preoccupied Mois and Negron barely looked up and gave brief nods. Alex stood there for a confused moment.

"Okay, take two: Am. I. *Right?*" he demanded again,

this time with both palms held out. Mois and Negron laughed in spite of themselves and reached over to slap his palms.

"Good work, Alex," Mois said. "I'm beginning to think you'd make a pretty good detective."

"Which is making me feel *really* threatened," Negron teased. "So please get back to your gigabytes or interfacing or whatever."

Gratified, Alex grinned widely as he returned to his workstation.

"Okay, sir," Negron said decisively. "We still have a lot of work to do to prove our case—against Garcia and *for* Hunter. The doctor is going to feel a lot differently when we bring this psycho to justice."

"I hope you're right."

Negron gathered individual papers from several files.

"We've traced some of Garcia's movements after he got fired from Creighton," she said. "He initially went to live in California—apparently with his parents. Shortly after, he declared bankruptcy...Then he went to Illinois. Records show that he got a license to prescribe controlled substances there. That has since lapsed...He then went Louisiana, but it doesn't look like he was there for very long."

She put her papers together with brisk efficiency. "I'd say that's not bad, considering we've had less than thirty-six hours. Oh, and I filed a warrant to get his cell phone records to find out where he is now. Murkowski should be receiving them any time."

Mois pulled one of the sheets from her pile and looked it over.

"This all tracks with what I found out," he said as he compared his own notes. "The HR manager at Creighton was able to pull up a lot of email correspondence relating to Garcia. She told me he applied for medical licenses in all three of those states you mentioned and—incredibly—kept giving Hunter as a reference. But every time the boards contacted the doctor he wouldn't give a recommendation. Garcia went to Louisiana for a consulting gig in the LSU psych division but he neglected to mention that he'd been fired from Creighton, which came up in a background check. So, they canned him."

"And Brumback?" Negron asked. "Was his involvement just cosigning the termination letter?"

"Dr. Brumback responded to a board inquiry about Garcia somewhere along the line. I'm guessing he probably also refused to give a recommendation."

Mois replaced the various documents and drummed his fingers on the table for a moment.

"I think the revenge plot was festering in Garcia's mind for years," Mois said thoughtfully. "He kept running into the same wall every time he tried to get a new job—that termination letter and no recommendations. Hunter was the primary motivator for his revenge plan. And in Garcia's thinking, he took care of the doctor by killing his son. Shirlee Sherman was probably just in the wrong place at the wrong time. But Garcia has continued to face those same exact rejections over the ensuing five years. So, he eventually needed to find another target for his frustrations: Dr. Brumback."

"Hey, Detective!" a voice called from across the room. Jim Murkowski waved from a table near the back. "Garcia's cell phone records just came through. The billing address is Terre Haute, Indiana."

All heads turned as Mois and Negron hurried over to the large wall map.

Negron pointed to two small yellow pins that had been stuck into areas inside the Omaha city limits. "The Hunter and Brumback residences."

"Okay, Jim, let's start with May 12, 2013," Mois said. "The day of the Brumback murders. Any activity on Garcia's phone?"

Murkowski scanned through the digital records. "Mmmm, yep! His phone pinged at a cell tower at 6842 North Forty-Fifth Street, near the Parkway."

Negron did a quick scan of the map and, finding the address, grabbed a red pin and pushed it in. It sat just below and to the left of the Brumback address.

"Not two miles from the cell tower!" Mois exclaimed.

"And it looks like Garcia did a few address searches that day," Murkowski said as he continued scrolling the records. "One was for 3436 Madera Lane."

"Someone do a check on that!" Mois called out, excitement rising in his voice as he scanned the map for the street. "Is it a residence or business?"

No more than two seconds passed before Alex shouted: "Residence! Dr. Chandra Bewtra."

At the name, Mois did a double-take and gripped Negron's arm. "Dr. Chandra Bewtra. Hunter mentioned her this morning. She also had a run-in with Garcia."

"Whoa—get this!" Alex exclaimed, his face buried in his monitor. "Bewtra reported an attempted break-in on *May 12, 2013*. Burglar alarm scared whoever it was off."

"That alarm probably saved her life!" Mois said as he strode purposefully up to the front of the room. Negron stared in amazement at the change in his demeanor from just a few minutes before. She hurried after him to the front of the room.

"What now?" she asked.

"Keep digging, build that case," Mois said as he quickly grabbed his laptop and briefcase. "And hold down the fort."

"And where are *you* going?" Negron demanded.

"Terre Haute."

CHAPTER 25

HE KEEPS HOPING I'M gonna leave. People just don't get that I know what they're thinking. They don't realize what I can do.

Anthony Garcia rapped the bottom of his glass on the warped countertop; the sound echoed loudly in the small, dimly lit bar. "Hey, how about putting on the news?"

The bartender looked up from the drinks he was mixing with a frown.

"I like keeping up with current events," Garcia said with a big friendly smile.

Sighing heavily, the aged bartender reached for the television remote and changed the channel from a ball game to the local news but—pointedly—kept the sound on mute. He noted that the weather forecast was being given, which meant that the main news was already over. *Maybe this weirdo with his dark, piercing eyes will take off after all,* the bartender thought. *This guy is trouble.*

Garcia toyed with his glass, whirling the last remaining

inch of whiskey around and around. He looked over at the only other two people in the bar: a young couple in stylish designer clothing sitting at the far end. They probably thought coming to this dive with its beat-up jukebox and missing floor tiles made them hip. Garcia thought about engaging them in conversation—just to see how uncomfortable he could make them. But he quickly realized it wouldn't take much and so wasn't really worth the effort.

Besides, he had bigger things on his mind. He'd missed the beginning of the news but he was sure the killings were still the top story. That was okay; he could wait until the ten o'clock broadcast. The bartender would really love that—four more hours of his company. He wondered if there'd be a new Crime Stoppers reward. There should be at least a $20,000 increase over the old one, he thought. After all, the body count had gone up—they could think of it as inflation.

Garcia giggled out loud—causing the young couple to glance at him with alarm. He just gave them his big smile and tipped his glass in their direction.

He remembered the first time he'd seen the Crime Stoppers reward flyer—the one that featured the drawing. It was like his own wanted poster, and he'd felt an enormous sense of pride at the sight of it. He really *was* a guy who got things done! He'd also felt—he had to admit—some fear. The sketch was startlingly accurate. But to his amazement, no one spotted him. And he'd wandered all over Omaha in the days that followed. Malls, grocery stores, movie theatres, bars—even the funeral! But no one recognized him. Or, maybe they'd never bothered to look at him in the first place.

It didn't matter. The important thing was he hadn't been caught. He'd been too smart for the police, not to mention the entire medical profession. None of them ever had the slightest idea who they were dealing with. But, he reasoned, it was inevitable that the pieces would start to fall together. Sooner or later even the dumb-shit police would realize who he was—and what he could do. And they'd be astonished, everyone would be.

Especially Mia.

She already knew he got things done for her. What she didn't know was how much more he planned to do—for both of them.

CHAPTER 26

ANTHONY GARCIA WASN'T A MONSTER.

He wasn't diabolically clever. He wasn't even particularly intelligent or skilled. He was just a cold-blooded killer who had been unusually lucky.

Up until now.

That was the conclusion Mois had reached after doing the eight-hour drive from Omaha to Terre Haute. He'd spent much of the trip trying to get inside the killer's head. What could drive a man, he wondered, to use murder as revenge for actions that his victims had played no part in, or—for that matter—had no awareness of?

Mois knew he was no psychologist, but as he entered the city limits of Terre Haute just after dawn, he realized that there probably was no mysterious secret behind Anthony Garcia. He was simply a weak, disturbed man who lashed out at others rather than accept the consequences of his own choices and actions.

"Get any sleep at your hotel, Detective?"

The words startled Mois out of his reverie. He was driving with Sergeant Martín Hidalgo of the Terre Haute Police Department. They were headed toward Garcia's residence, three squad cars followed immediately behind them. It was a warm, sunny day and Hidalgo had the car's AC at nearly full blast. It seemed like overkill to Mois but he was glad; the chill was helping keep him awake.

"I got about forty-five minutes' shut-eye before my cell rang," Mois answered, stifling a yawn. "My son—reminding me about his rugby game on Saturday. If I miss it, I think he's going to file for legal emancipation."

Hidalgo laughed knowingly. Mois figured the sergeant to be in his early forties. His eyebrows and goatee were jet-black and impeccably trimmed; on top of that, he was wearing a striking Hugo Boss suit. Mois thought Hidalgo looked as immaculately groomed and alert as he felt disheveled and weary.

"I get what you're saying. It's the damned job," Hidalgo said. "I've missed my share of my daughter's soccer games. And every time I do, her future wedding budget gets just a little bit bigger."

The sergeant turned off the freeway they'd been on and entered what looked to be a slightly run-down middle-class neighborhood.

"Our department has had a few run-ins with your Mr. Garcia," Hidalgo said in a more serious tone. "Apparently, some college kids—three girls—live across the street from his house. He's done some disturbing things—once brought them flowers in the middle of the night, so drunk he could barely stand. And one girl alleges that he's peeped in her bedroom window. Also, Chicago PD picked him up on a DUI a few months back."

They pulled into a neighborhood of homes that dated from the early 1950s, mostly small, nondescript bungalows. While a few looked like they had been upgraded or at least well maintained over the years, the majority were on the shoddy side. Hidalgo stopped the car directly in front of Garcia's address, a plain white house. Two of the other patrol cars parked at dramatic angles in the middle of the street to block exit or entrance. They immediately began flashing their patrol lights. Hidalgo noted Mois's surprised look.

"I'm thinking a show of force might be good for Mr. Garcia," Hidalgo noted. "We've got back-up the next street over. He isn't going anywhere."

The two men approached the house; one of the other officers—a jocky-looking guy named Ben Bateman—followed close behind. Mois thought that while the residence looked a little dingy and the lawn needed mowing, overall it was more presentable than he would have imagined. He wondered if Garcia would seem just as bland and unremarkable when he finally met him face-to-face.

"Records show that the house is facing foreclosure," Hidalgo noted. He then suddenly and fiercely banged a fist on the front door. The startling sound jolted through the otherwise quiet neighborhood, just as the sergeant had intended. The inside of house remained silent. After a beat, Hidalgo put a hand on the door knob and turned it.

The door opened. The three men looked at each other in surprise.

"*Anthony Garcia? Terre Haute Police!*" Batemen boomed. His voice echoed emptily through the house. They waited for a response, then Hidalgo warily led the way inside.

Mois immediately noted that the interior wasn't much different from the outside. Not dirty but not clean, with inexpensive furniture that was mismatched but not threadbare. On the left side of the front hall was a small den with a desk and a file cabinet. Files and papers were haphazardly stacked on the desk, chair, and floor. Mois walked in and picked up a sheet while Hidalgo and Batemen proceeded to investigate the rest of the house.

Mois was flipping through a few pages when Hidalgo reentered.

"All's clear," he said. "I'm thinking Mr. Garcia may have vacated the premises."

Mois nodded and read aloud from one of the sheets: "For my parents, in case of emergency...He's got his mortgage statements here. Life insurance policy. He's definitely trying to get his personal effects in order."

Just then, Bateman called from the back of the house: "Sergeant! Got something!"

Mois and Hidalgo hurried down a small hallway and entered what seemed to be the master bedroom. Clothes were strewn all over the floor and the bed was unmade. The dresser drawers had all been left sitting open. Bateman pointed to the top drawer. Mois stepped forward and looked inside. Sitting there was an empty box for a 9mm pistol.

"That model fits the magazine we found at one of the crime scenes," Mois noted. As Bateman started to carefully bag the evidence, Mois looked over the rest of the room. Spying something under the bed, he bent down and retrieved a legal-sized notepad. Hidalgo looked over Mois's shoulder.

"What is it?" he asked.

"Some kind of journal, I think," Mois said as he flipped through the pages. Wild scrawling covered some sheets, while others contained neatly ordered lists. On one page a single line was repeated several times. "*If you wrong us, shall we not revenge?*" Mois read in a mystified tone.

"Shakespeare," Hidalgo said without missing a beat. "From *The Merchant of Venice.*"

Mois couldn't help but do a double-take at the sergeant's unexpected literary knowledge. Hidalgo shrugged.

"I did some theater in college," he said in a low voice. "And if you tell anyone on the force, I'll have your car impounded for a month."

"I'm not sure if I'm more surprised that Garcia knew the quote or that you did." Mois laughed. He turned the next page and saw another list. This one had several names on it. And two of them had dark lines struck across them.

Those names were Dr. William Hunter and Dr. Roger Brumback.

Below, there were two other names: Dr. Charlotte

DeLavigne and Dr. Chandra Bewtra. They did *not* have lines struck through them.

"What's that?" Hidalgo asked.

Mois slowly looked up at the sergeant.

"A hit list."

CHAPTER 27

"OH SWEETIE...YOU'RE JUST way too *nice* for me," Mia said as she backed her hips in between Red's stumpy spread legs. "I only date, you know, *bad boys.*"

She wriggled her butt suggestively and then quickly pivoted away before he could touch her. Mia had given enough lap dances to know how to outmaneuver even the most inappropriate and drunken client. She'd offered Red this free session as a thank-you for getting her son's medication last week. She very much hoped it would settle their account, so to speak, and that there'd be no more talk of a date. But Red had brought it up the moment they entered one of the club's tiny private rooms. Mia had tried to laugh it off. He was clearly not only very drunk but also strangely zonked out, and Mia suspected he was on something. After all, he had access to prescription meds.

As the low lights in the room flickered along with a change in the music tempo, Mia tried doing one of her signature gyrations to distract Red from talking but he leaned forward and grabbed her forearm.

"You *are* going out with me! You're my girl," he said angrily in an unexpected shout. His yell was so loud that Mia was afraid he'd attract attention. She'd tipped Eddie, the security guard, twenty dollars not to log this dance and not to tell JJ, the surly club manager. She realized she needed to calm Red down and get him out of here as quickly as possible.

"Now don't be silly, sweetie," Mia said in what she hoped sounded like playful manner as she did a bump-and-grind. "I mean, I don't even know your *name*!"

At that, he stood up from the club chair and staggered toward her. His eyes were suddenly dark and piercing. Mia reflexively backed away from him.

"*Everyone* knows who I am!" he bellowed as he grabbed at her. "But they don't know how *bad* I am. You have no idea what I *do* when people cross me!"

Mia felt a ripple of fear shoot down her spine. She knew Eddie was within shouting distance, he'd be in the room in a flash if she called out. For now, she didn't really doubt her safety. But for the first time she realized that Red wasn't just the lonely drunk she'd taken him for; a skeevy guy, to be sure, but essentially harmless. No, there was something wrong with this guy—something *seriously* wrong.

"Okay, okay honey, just chill," Mia said, trying to be soothing but aware that her voice was shaking slightly. "Let's just have a good time here, all right? Just sit down. We can talk after I dance. Just relax for now."

To her surprise, Red immediately obeyed; he resumed his seat like a chastened schoolboy. He stared as she warily started dancing again and suddenly gave her the smile he always wore when he watched her out front. A friendly, dopey kind of smile. Maybe this was going to turn out all right, Mia thought with relief. Yeah, okay, the guy is drunk and a little high—that's no crime. Especially in this place.

"I killed a boy once. An eleven-year-old," Red said in a normal speaking voice that was somehow more chilling than his previous shouting. "And a couple of older people. Stabbed them. You can't get any badder than that, right?"

Mia couldn't help herself—she froze on the spot. This wasn't happening—this guy couldn't be serious. As she paused, the look in Red's eyes changed again. They went back to being dark and beady—and angry. He locked his gaze onto Mia's. It was as though he was daring her to believe him—or *dis*believe him. She couldn't tell which—she only knew that she was, after all, absolutely in danger.

"Well, you—you're being *bad* because you aren't appreciating my dancing!" she said, her voice quavering. "Maybe we'll do this another time, okay, hon? I gotta be out front soon anyway."

Mia turned and picked up the sheer baby-doll dress she always wore when at the bar. But before she knew what was happening, Red jumped up and tore the dress away from her. Twisting it in his hands, he backed her up against the wall of the small room, using his body to block any chance she had of getting to the door. She could now smell the alcohol on him—it seemed to ooze out of his pores and from his breath.

"You don't have to dance anymore," he said with strange eagerness, his eyes burning with a crazed kind of glee. "You'll come with me. We're going to Louisiana!"

At this point, Mia didn't care if JJ did fire her for giving a free lap dance. She just wanted out of this room, away from this unhinged guy. She was about to scream for Eddie when, suddenly, Red unclenched his grip on her dress. He gingerly shook the material out and then held it up to her. He nodded for her to put it on. Wide-eyed with fear, Mia slowly slipped the dress over her head and let it fall down around her hips.

Swaying unsteadily, Red reached out and awkwardly petted the folds so that the dress flowed evenly. Mia held her breath, unsure what was happening now, what had caused his mood to swing again so drastically. As he looked her over, Red's big, dopey smile returned—and all of the threat seemed to vanish from his face.

"I'll go first," he said, his words slurred but intent. "You'll come later. Once everything is done, I'll send for you."

He slowly backed away from her—still with that wide, weirdly delighted grin on his face. Though he was looking directly at her, Mia felt like he was seeing something just beyond her; a reality all his own.

After he walked out the door, she stood there, stunned. She struggled to find a way to steady her panicked breathing.

Suddenly, the door swung back open. Mia yelped out loud but it was just Eddie—the short but powerfully built security guard wearing his signature red bandana and Hoosiers tank top.

"Move it, baby!" he whispered urgently. "JJ is lookin' for ya—and he's out for blood! He switched the dancing order and put you up next!"

Mia just continued standing there, white-faced and trembling, unable to say a word.

Eddie gave her a curious look. "It's okay, I got your back. I told JJ you were just gettin' something out of your car. He's cool now. But girl, you got *no* idea how close you just came to gettin' *killed*!"

CHAPTER 28

IT WAS BEGINNING TO feel almost physical to Mois: the sense of getting closer and closer to Anthony Garcia.

Five long, frustrating years. Years spent going over and *over* the evidence and the baffling lack of motive. And, finally, a portrait of the killer of Tom Hunter and Shirlee Sherman was coming into focus. He was no longer an abstract theory, an out-there possibility, a desperate guess. Anthony Garcia was a flesh-and-blood person, and his weaknesses and vulnerabilities were leading the task force to him with the precision of a GPS tracking device.

Hey, that's not a bad line, Mois thought to himself. *I gotta remember to use it with the team.*

Despite how tired he'd been the previous day, he'd had another night of very little sleep in his nondescript hotel room. He couldn't get Garcia out of his mind. And he kept worrying about how he was going to keep the task force back in Omaha focused and motivated while he worked remotely from Hidalgo's small, stark office at the Terre Haute Police Department.

The sergeant was now at his desk, tapping away at his keyboard. Again, Hidalgo looked perfectly groomed, like a detective in a glossy studio film. Mois felt like his sad sidekick; always overtired and underdressed in comparison.

"Okay, we're up," Hidalgo said with a nod.

Mois came around to the side of his desk and took a seat, the two large men squeezing together so that they could both view Hidalgo's computer monitor. A Skype call image sputtered on the screen and suddenly Negron's face came into view.

"Good afternoon, gentlemen," she said, sounding tinny and remote from the Omaha task force room. "I look terrible on this, don't I?"

"You're beautiful. You could literally charge us for this call," Mois said jokingly.

"You heard that blatant sexual harassment, right, Sergeant Hidalgo?" Negron fired back.

"Yep, I'm recording this," Hidalgo said. "Demand a raise or I'll release it to the media."

Just then someone off-camera said something to Negron. Mois could see only a portion of the room behind her but from the background chatter it was clear that the team was still hard at work.

Negron listened and nodded, then turned back to the screen.

"Big news, Mois," she said. "Remember that attempted

burglary on Dr. Bewtra's home the same day as the Brumback killings? We ran a comparison on a DNA sample that was taken off her door and it's a match for what we got at the Brumbacks'."

"Excellent!" Mois said. "We got some news on this end, too. A very scared woman called into the station this morning. Works at a local gentlemen's club. A regular customer came in last night and boasted about stabbing an eleven-year-old boy. The woman's description of the man matches Garcia perfectly."

"So, we know he's likely been in the Terre Haute area within the last eight to ten hours," Hidalgo chimed in. "We put a watch on his house, but he didn't show last night."

Mois leaned in toward the screen. "Garcia's home is facing foreclosure, he can't get a job, and we saw evidence that he's putting his personal effects in order. He must know we're getting close. This is a guy who has come to the end of the line. He's got nothing to lose. I want everyone to keep that in mind."

Negron was about to say something when suddenly Alex Burns popped his head into the frame.

"Yo, Detective!" he said. "Hey, I tracked that doctor— Charlotte DeLavigne. She works at—"

Negron abruptly pushed Alex away from the screen. "*Hello?* I'm talking here!"

She grabbed the paper Alex had been holding and began reading. "Looks like Dr. DeLavigne works at Louisiana State U in the—"

"Let me guess," Mois said. "The psychiatric division."

Negron nodded. "Yep. And she it seems she has some very clear recollections of her encounters with Anthony Garcia, all negative."

"Let's give a heads-up to the Baton Rouge PD," Mois said. "There's a very good chance Garcia plans to return there."

"You got it," Negron agreed. "Oh, and I've put out a four-state alert on Garcia's Honda. He won't—"

Negron sighed in irritation as yet another person said something to her from the background. She then leaned over to the right, listening intently to whatever the person was saying. Mois suddenly became aware that the chatter in the background had stopped—something was clearly up, something important. Negron urgently turned back to the screen.

"Murkowski says Garcia's cell phone has been reactivated!" she exclaimed. "We've got a signal...Garcia is traveling south—looks like he's on I-57...just outside of Effingham, Illinois."

"That hooks up to I-55," Hidalgo said. "And then it's just a straight shot down to Louisiana!"

Mois and Hidalgo were up and out of their chairs so quickly it seemed to Negron that they'd literally evaporated from her screen.

"*Hey!*" she yelled into her monitor's camera. "*Call me from the road!*"

Negron waited for some kind of response but none came. She frowned in disappointment at the image of the two empty chairs that stared back at her. She felt put out—not only, she realized, by the men's abrupt exit but at missing the climax of the Garcia case.

She sighed and went to turn off the Skype chat app when suddenly Mois's face reappeared on her screen.

"We did it, Negron," he said, leaning down into the camera. "Five years of disappointments and dead-end leads. Long nights and frustrating days. But it's coming together. We're going to nail Anthony Garcia to the wall, the floor, and the ceiling. Couldn't have done it without ya. Just wanted you to know that."

He held up his hand and pressed it against the screen. Negron smiled and pressed her hand up in response.

"Go get him, pardner."

CHAPTER 29

THE LIST HAD GROWN so short. It was almost disconcerting how little there was left to do. Anthony Garcia had never doubted that he'd get to the end. But the funny thing was, the list had occupied him for so long he'd never given much thought to what he'd do once he was finished, when the slate was wiped clean.

After Baton Rouge, maybe he would head to Mexico. The warm weather would be a nice change after so many years in the chilly Midwest. He'd get a place near the ocean. Mia would like that. Everything was easier in Mexico—everybody knew that. He could probably even get some kind of medical license down there. You could buy anything in Mexico—even job references.

The images of this new life just past the horizon made Garcia smile. It was a warm night and it was pleasant to be gliding down the uncrowded freeway. He felt a growing excitement that his destination was getting closer and closer. But he was in no hurry. As always, the timing had to be just right.

He reached across the front seat for his flask. He noticed it felt light; he'd have to stop for a refill soon. He took a long swig and, as the whiskey warmed his throat, went back to visualizing his future in the blazing sun.

But a flash of light interrupted that image, and it was followed a screeching siren. A patrol car had appeared out of nowhere just behind him. Garcia glanced at his odometer. Shit, he'd been flying at eighty-five miles per hour! He'd been too lost in thought to even notice.

Garcia slowed but didn't pull over. He had to think this through. Nothing was going to stop him from doing what he had to do—*nothing*.

The patrol car's loudspeaker angrily boomed: "Pull over to the side of the freeway *immediately*!"

Garcia slowed more, hesitated, then finally pulled onto the shoulder. He glanced up in his rearview mirror and watched as the patrol car pulled in about fifteen feet behind him. Nothing happened for a moment. Garcia figured it was a state trooper and that he was probably calling in the Honda's license plate.

Though it was very dark, the passing headlights of other drivers slowing down to check out the off-road drama occasionally illuminated the side of the freeway. When the trooper finally exited his car, Garcia saw that he was a large, broad-shouldered man. As he approached, he spoke into a microphone on his lapel. He then slowly came up to the car window.

"License and registration, please."

The man's voice was deep and curt. Garcia stared up

at him—for some reason he wasn't able to completely make out the trooper's features. The passing headlights didn't help, they backlit the hulking figure outside of his window. Garcia blinked a few times and tried to squint.

"Have you been drinking, sir?"

"Since—since I was fourteen," Garcia stuttered. It was a line that had always gotten a laugh before, maybe he hadn't said it the right way. He was suddenly feeling kind of woozy. He knew the trooper was staring at him.

He also knew he wasn't about to let himself be arrested.

He thought about his gun.

Almost as an afterthought, he had tucked it into his waistband before hitting the road. He'd half forgotten about it. But now he could feel the cool metal pressing against his stomach. How quickly could he reach for it? Should he grab it by pretending to go for his wallet?

"I need to see your license and registration, sir."

Garcia realized his hands were still gripping the steering wheel. Could he hit the gas and just take off? How far could he get? How much time would he have before the patrol car caught up?

Out of the corner of his eye, Garcia saw the trooper slowly reach for the gun on his hip. Would he draw? Could Garcia grab his gun a split-second faster?

As Garcia sat there deliberating, he commended himself on how calm he was being, despite his hazy head. Others in a similar situation would panic. But not Anthony Garcia. Not someone who had done what he had.

What did he really have to lose? he asked himself. He'd risk having one item on his list go unchecked. But hadn't he already accomplished so much? He'd settled the scores that meant the most. No one could say he hadn't gotten things done.

"Sir?"

The trooper quietly undid the snap of his gun holder. Garcia turned and looked up at him with a big, friendly smile.

"Would it be okay if I reached for my wallet?" he asked politely. "Or would you rather I got out my car registration first?"

The trooper hesitated. Though his face was still shadowed, Garcia could tell he was staring bullets at him. The two men were testing each other. Who would make the first move—and what would it be?

Suddenly another flash of lights raked across the scene. Startled, the trooper looked to the side as another patrol car came screeching to halt just beside them. Using the distraction, Garcia grabbed for his gun. The slick metal felt amazingly powerful and reassuring as his fingers gripped the handle.

But his head must have been woozier than he'd realized. Time seemed to have either slowed down or speeded up on him. He couldn't tell which—all he knew was that the precious split-second advantage he'd been given had disappeared.

He was only touching his gun while the trooper's was aimed at the side of his head.

"*Freeze!* If you so much as blink I will fire," the trooper said with quiet ferocity.

Garcia stared straight ahead. He didn't move. He didn't say a word.

Dimly, he became aware of other voices outside the car. And then the door opened and someone pried the gun from under his belt. They yanked him out of the car, but Garcia didn't struggle; he moved robotically. Another person started speaking, someone other than the trooper.

"I am Detective Derek Mois of the Omaha Police Department," the man said tersely. "And I am arresting you for the murders of Thomas Hunter, Shirlee Sherman, and Roger and Mary Brumback. You have the right to remain silent..."

The detective droned on and on. But Garcia tuned him out. Other words filled his ears. A phrase, something he had read long ago that had stuck with him, repeated in his mind.

If you wrong us, shall we not revenge?

That was it. He had done what was necessary. He had shown the world who Anthony Garcia was. He could hold his head up high to these cops as well as to the lawyers and reporters and doctors who would come.

But, as he was led in handcuffs to the trooper's patrol car, he suddenly felt strangely deflated. Why? He had demanded and gotten retribution, even when innocent people like that housekeeper had stood in his way. He had never faltered. Then why did he now feel so...empty?

If you wrong us, shall we not revenge?

The patrol car's siren screeched to life and the trooper floored the engine. The vehicle shot down freeway. But in the backseat, the shackled Anthony Garcia barely noticed. He couldn't stop wondering something: after all that he had done—all the debts collected and all the points proven—what kind of achievements were they when, in the end, he'd never had any other choice?

EPILOGUE

October 26, 2016

"THE JURY FINDS THE defendant, Anthony Joseph Garcia, guilty of first-degree murder."

There was no reaction in the courtroom: no gasps of surprise, no murmurs of approval, no shouts of outrage. The lawyers, the judge, the jury, and the spectators all remained silent while the foreman read through the lengthy four-count guilty verdict. The quiet didn't surprise Mois. He had witnessed this type of stillness many times in courtrooms; he often thought of it as a show of respect for the victims.

Even so, there was definitely something unusual about the silence of the defendant.

Anthony Garcia sat at the defense table with a blank look on his face, just as he had for months; his thoughts seemingly far, far away. He had never once said a word, not even when the judge directly questioned him. His lawyers had complained that their client refused to speak to them for the entirety of the trial. They had tried to use it as grounds for proof of insanity.

Finally, the judge closed the proceedings by noting that Garcia was eligible for the death penalty. But he announced that he was delaying sentencing until Garcia underwent psychiatric testing. The prisoner's ultimate fate—whether he would spend the remainder of his life behind bars in a psych ward or on death row—would be determined at a future date.

Garcia remained stoic, apparently disinterested. Only when two heavily armed guards led him out of the courtroom did the palpable tension in the room finally lift.

As the crowd began to disperse, Mois felt a hand on his arm.

"Detective Mois, we just want to say thank you one last time."

William and Claire Hunter, dressed in somber dark suits, had changed a great deal in the eight years since their son's murder. They looked older, of course, but Mois noted an even more significant change from the last time he'd seen them. It was in their faces—they no longer had that baffled, stricken look. Mois knew the pain of their son's death would be with them for the rest of their lives. But it seemed the arrest and now the verdict had, at last, brought them some sense of peace.

"You told me, many years ago, that you would never give up looking for my son's killer," Hunter said as he shook Mois's hand. "You kept your word. We are so grateful."

Mois chatted with the couple for a few minutes. They were sorry to learn that Detective Negron was away on a case and asked Mois to relate their appreciation of her efforts. Future plans were discussed; the Hunters reported that they were finally both retiring and heading for a milder climate. After a moment, hands were again warmly shaken; though no one said it, they all knew it was unlikely they would ever meet again.

After the couple headed out the door, Mois stopped by the prosecutors' table and congratulated the lawyers. They insisted the detective and his team's investigative work had all but done their job for them.

Checking his watch, Mois finally turned toward the courtroom door—and saw Teresa Negron standing against the doorjamb, her arms casually folded across her chest.

"*What?* I thought you were in St. Louis till next week!" Mois said, surprised and pleased at the sight of her.

"And miss seeing Garcia go down? Oh, *helllll* no!" she said with mock attitude.

"I'm glad. The Hunters asked me to thank you."

She nodded. "I just spoke with them. Such nice people. It's horrible that they had to go through this—any of it."

Together, they walked out of the courtroom and down the grand marble-tiled hallway. When they came out of the exit doors, the two paused on the courthouse steps to take in the gloriously bright, sunny autumn morning.

"Hey, I've meaning to give you props on the new DNA evidence that came in on the Blanchard case," Mois said. "I'd say you deserve a cigarette for that one."

"Aw, I had to give them up for good once I made detective. I was having too many successes," Negron laughed.

Mois chuckled but gave her a curious look. "You told me once—in *no* uncertain terms—that you were eventually going to get Craig Talley. How were you so sure it was him?"

Negron thought for a moment and then shrugged. "Sometimes you just *know*. And then there are those other times—like this Garcia case—when it seems like no matter what you do or how hard you dig, you're *never* going to know who did it. Or why."

"It's a hell of a profession, Terry," Mois sighed.

"*What* were we thinking?" she asked ruefully.

Mois started to say something but then suddenly raised his arm and pointed. Across the lush grounds surrounding the courthouse, a lone couple was walking slowly toward the parking lot. They were holding hands and, after a moment, the woman rested her head on the man's shoulder. Leaning over, William Hunter affectionately rubbed his cheek against his wife Claire's short white hair.

Mois and Negron glanced at each other and smiled.

"We were thinking about days like this."

"Amen, pardner."

DET. HARRIET BLUE IS BACK.

BUT WHEN HER BROTHER IS ACCUSED OF MURDER, WILL SHE SELF-DESTRUCT?

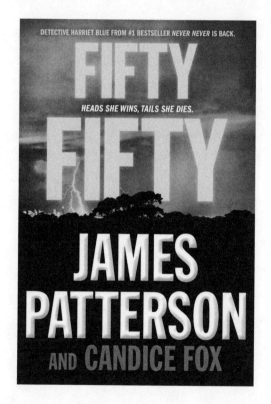

DETECTIVE HARRIET BLUE FROM #1 BESTSELLER *NEVER NEVER* IS BACK.

FIFTY

HEADS SHE WINS, TAILS SHE DIES.

FIFTY

JAMES PATTERSON

AND CANDICE FOX

Please turn the page for a preview.

CHAPTER 1

SHE WAS PERFECT. And so rarely the perfect ones came, fluttering out of the darkness like moths into golden light. Swift and uncatchable.

He had wandered the third floor of the car park for a couple of hours now, risking it all for his ideal victim. A number of young women had crossed the little grassy field below where he stood as classes at the university ended and new ones began. He watched them toting shoulder bags and the occasional paper coffee cup, blinking in the warm daylight. Then the place was deserted again, and he waited.

It was bright out, leaving a dark shadow in the corner of the parking lot, to the right of the fire stairs. He'd watched a potential girl enter the stairwell, his heart thumping, but she was only halfway up the concrete steps toward him before he realized she wasn't right. She had a friend on the phone. Cackling laughter. No. He'd know her when he saw her. Big doe eyes. Frightened, down-turned mouth. Thin wrists he could squeeze and twist.

The desire to flee picked at him. It was risky, hanging

around too long. The university campus was on high alert after the police had found his previous works. Marissa. Elle. Rosetta. His brunette beauties mangled, ruined. Tragedies laid out on the sand. As news of the Georges River Killer spread, girls across campus had started dyeing and cutting their hair, walking in groups at night, having the security guards take them to their cars. It wasn't about the hair for him—although he hadn't failed to notice their striking resemblance to his first, many years ago. No, his university girls had simply been the right kind of in-nocent. Content, confident. He looked for the forthright stride, the high chin, the captive excitement of rosebuds just before they bloom.

He told himself to be patient. The plan had gone so well so far. His finale was worth the risk. A few more minutes. He wandered into the stairwell as he heard footsteps.

Then he saw her, her hand on the rail, gripping, pulling as she ascended. A slice of her soft cream brow and high cheekbone as she turned the corner.

Oh, there she was. His perfect girl.

CHAPTER 2

SHE EMERGED FROM the stairwell door and he swept an arm around her throat, yanked her backwards. The sickening rush of chemicals through his veins threatened to knock him off balance. She didn't make a sound at first. The breath left her instantly. Her bag fell. Then the clap of his palm over her mouth, her heels dragging as he turned and pulled her toward his vehicle.

"No!" a muffled wail. "Stop! Stop! Stop!"

She bucked, twisted, tried to sink out of his arms. He was ready for the movement, knew the victim's dance by heart. He sank with her, gripped tighter, pulled her body hard against his. Never letting her think for a moment that she had a hope of escape. Hope was a dangerous thing.

He had no idea where it came from. She was totally under his control. But hope *had* infected her, as tangible in her body as an electric pulse. Without warning she stiffened, let go of his hands and swung her fists over her own head at his face.

A fumbling blow. The shock of it. He let her go. She hit the ground and the scream erupted out of her, rapturous, like a song. He punched her in the stomach, tried to gather her up. This wasn't the plan!

She twisted and scrambled against a car. He swiped at her. Missed.

She was up and running. And as she ran, she almost knocked over another girl standing there watching, mouth hanging open, phone in hand.

"Run!" his victim screamed at the girl, already disappearing into the fire stairs. "Run!"

He righted himself. The new girl was too shocked, appalled by what she'd witnessed, to take a step back out of range. Big brown eyes, dark skin, the slowly opening and closing mouth of a woman feeling paralyzing terror wash over her.

She wasn't his perfect girl, but she was a delightful surprise.

He seized her wrist.

CHAPTER 3

SHE FIRST BECAME aware of the television in the corner, its robotic noises, bleeping and zooming and piercing jingles, the crash and tumble of advertisements. Caitlyn shifted her face against the mattress. She was sweating badly, or bleeding, she couldn't tell. She tried to speak and found her lips were sealed by tape. Panic shot through her. A spike of pain that reached from the heel of her bare foot to the crown of her skull. She turned, struggled against the tape on her wrists. Her nose was broken.

A damp concrete room. A bare mattress, a blanket bunched at the end. Rusty beer kegs and wooden crates, a pile of trash in the corner waist high. Mop heads and buckets and a milk crate full of bottles, a vacuum cleaner covered in an inch of dust. Caitlyn reeled, tried to get her bearings, scrabbled against the wall. Her ankles were bound. The terror was so loud in her brain that for a moment it blocked out all sound from the television. She saw him standing before the screen, turned away from her, his hands hanging by his sides.

The university. The car park. She'd been on the phone

to her mother in California, fending off her ridiculous warnings about the killer on campus. It had been bright. Sunny. Afternoon. Then, in a snap, a different picture altogether, the curtain sailing closed and sailing open again on a horror-movie scene. The girl fighting with the hooded figure between the cars, rushing past her, a blur of heat. *Run! Run!* Caitlyn hadn't run. Hadn't done anything. And then he'd been right in front of her, impossibly fast, his fist swinging down toward her face.

Every story she'd ever heard of abduction and death and rape rushed through her mind, a whole catalogue of atrocities collected since she was a child and her teacher first taught them about Stranger Danger. True crime novels she'd browsed in airports. Macabre, late-night episodes of *SVU*, young girls being dragged out of sex dungeons, recounting atrocities, shivering in the witness stand. *Now you are one of them*, Caitlyn thought. *Now your nightmare begins.*

The man in front of the television was angry. His broad shoulders were high. She watched, wild-eyed, as he gripped the back of his shaven skull, ran a hand down his neck and back again, scratched hard. Caitlyn looked at the television screen just beyond him, the police leading a cuffed, black-haired man toward a waiting paddy wagon.

"*...the arrest of Samuel Jacob Blue over the murders of three young women abducted from the area surrounding the University of Sydney campus. Police say Blue was apprehended in...*"

"This wasn't the plan," the man with the shaved head

murmured. He turned and glanced at Caitlyn where she sat huddled against the wall. He seemed to be assessing, his mind churning with decisions. "Fuck. Fuck!"

The rage rippled through him. She saw it creep up his arms until his neck tightened, the thick jugular standing out against sweat-sheened skin.

He turned and watched the screen and gripped his head again. "It wasn't finished yet!" Caitlyn watched as he knelt, almost shakily, before the screen. His fingers twitched, inches away from the glass, as Samuel Jacob Blue appeared, glancing fearfully at the crowd as the paddy wagon doors closed on him.

"I need you," her captor said, his eyes locked on Blue. "I need you, Sam."

CHAPTER 4

Four months later...

FOUR MONTHS. ONE hundred and twenty-seven days, to be exact. That's how long my brother had been in prison for a crime he did not commit. I stood on the steps of the courthouse, ignoring my partner, trying to decide if my math was correct. It was. As I waited, staring down at my ridiculous high heels, listening to the shouts of the crowd nearby, another day of Sam's life was being lost. I drew hard on my cigarette, clutched the stupid pink handbag into my side. The passing seconds were agony. Waiting for the court to open once again on the circus that was the Georges River Killer case. Another day I would fail to bring him home.

I am a Sex Crimes detective with the Sydney police. I used to think I was pretty good at my job. Versatile. Adaptable. I had a keen sense for bad men, and I wasn't afraid of bending the rules to make them admit what they were. A cracked tooth here, a broken finger there. I made men tremble in their seats. Harriet Blue: Terror at Five-Foot Two. While I was the natural enemy of the caged rape suspect, I could also be soft and gentle enough to coax a tiny, bruised child into revealing what his or her abuser had done, when no amount of coddling and bargaining by trained psychologists had struck pay dirt.

But, four months earlier, my own colleagues had left the police station where I worked on their way to make the biggest arrest of their careers—a man they believed was a vicious serial killer who had tortured and murdered three university students. No amount of intuition, or skill, or training had prepared me for the fact that that man was my own flesh and blood.

Sam's case was all the nation was talking about. The newspapers were calling him Australia's worst serial killer, and that was no small claim—every article compared him with the fiends who'd taken up the mantle before him. Ivan Milat, the Backpacker Murderer. Arnold Sodeman, the Schoolgirl Strangler. Eric Edgar Cooke, the Night Caller. Now came Samuel Jacob Blue, the Georges River Killer, responsible for the prolonged, brutal deaths of three beautiful, young students.

For four months, I'd been determined to do everything right to help my brother go free. He was innocent. I was sure of it. The man who abducted, raped, tortured and strangled the three women I saw every night on the news was not the man who'd once been a boy snuggled beside me in the temporary beds at the offices of the Department of Children's Services. He was not that terrified boy, whispering to me in the dark, wondering which foster home we were going to be shipped to next. He was not the teenager who'd defended me at various high schools when the kids came to pick on the shabby interlopers. The one who made me birthday cards when our new families forgot. Whoever he was, he did not have my brother's soulful kindness. His never-ending generosity.

On the footpath nearby, the usual gathering of gawkers and court ghouls waited for the doors to open. One caught my eye and spat on the ground, spoke loudly to his friend in the queue.

"She knew what he was up to," he said. "How could she not?"

"Don't listen, Harry." My partner, Detective Edward Whittacker, tried to take my arm and turn me away from the crowd. "You'll only make yourself madder."

"I'm not mad," I lied, shrugging him off. "I'm cool. I'm calm. Today's going to be the day. We'll find it today. The key."

I'd been talking about the "key' to my brother's case since his arrest. The thing that freed him. A piece of false testimony. A surprise witness. Something, anything. I'd been looking into Sam's case, and I hadn't found the key that proved he wasn't the killer. But I had high hopes. Hell, my hopes got so high sometimes I had fantasies of the killer himself walking into the courtroom and confessing. Giving up was far from my mind.

I spotted my brother's prosecutor, the enormous, broad-shouldered Liam Woolfmyer, strolling toward us with a colleague beside him. Whitt had my arm again, his other hand fumbling at his necktie.

"Don't say a word," he growled.

"You keep pawing at me and it'll be more than words you have to worry about."

"I'm warning you, Harry." Whitt glared over the top of his glasses at me. The gentle, fastidious detective had been mortified to hear me sneer a stream of obscenities at Woolfmyer the first morning of my brother's hearings.

Sometimes there's a wild Harriet in me, a woman I can't control. She rears her ugly head without warning. The comment from the queue already had her twitching. But then I stole a glance at Woolfmyer, and the worst of all things happened. He locked eyes with me, smiled, and leaned over in mock confidence to his companion.

"Samuel Blue won't last a single night in Long Bay prison," Woolfmyer said. "He's far too pretty. Someone will make him their bitch."

The bad Harriet in me swelled, like white-hot steam, blinding and painful behind my eyes. As Woolfmyer passed I was already taking steps to catch up with him. I barely heard Whitt's call.

The few meters between Woolfmyer and me closed in an instant. I was behind him. My hand reaching up, completely beyond my control.

I tapped him on the shoulder. Woolfmyer stopped and turned.

I punched him as hard as I could in the temple.

CHAPTER 5

I'VE ALWAYS BEEN a fighter. It's necessary, when you have a childhood like mine, to know how to defend yourself physically. I was a scrappy, dirty fighter before my police chief taught me how to box. He made the mistake of honing the self-taught craft of a brutal, remorseless combatant. Size means nothing when you know what you're doing. I swung up and to the left with a hard, balled right fist and smashed the prosecutor with all the force in my arm, shoulder and hip.

The only sound was the dull thump of his body on the pavement, the whisper of his settling robes, a big bird brought down out of the sky by a rifle blast.

My regret was instant. I looked around. Woolfmyer's friend staggering back. Whitt nearby, his hand still out, reaching, desperate. The crowd, a huddle of journalists. Horror and guilt rushed up through my body. Cameras flashed.

I felt a bizarre impulse to reach down and help the unconscious lawyer to his feet. To brush him off, slap him on the back, pretend it was all going to be OK.

But everything was far from OK. The police officer who had been guarding the front doors of the courthouse began to march toward me, taking his cuffs from his belt.

CHAPTER 6

I STOOD IN the entrance to the holding cell and stared at the women there. They were like lazy, uninterested cats lounging on the steel benches. One girl was lying on her belly on the floor, a magazine spread out before her. There were more magazines in a stack on one of the benches, trashy celebrity rags. An adult slumber party in a concrete bedroom. A gaggle of arrested shoplifters, prostitutes, drug runners. I went to the nearest bench and sat down, put my face in my hands as the steel door slammed shut.

I guessed a lot of women who ended up in a cell at the Parramatta Police headquarters thought what I was thinking in that moment. That their lives were over. That they'd had some fuck-ups in their lifetime, sure, but this was a whole new level of idiocy. Holding cells are where mistakes are offered up for evaluation. This is it. This is where all a person's chickens come home to roost.

Detective Inspector Nigel Spader was at the door to the holding cell now as I sat cracking my aching knuckles.

He leaned on the wall and looked through the bars at me, folding his hairy ginger arms.

"Harriet," he said. "What a mess you've got yourself in."

Spader had spearheaded the case against my brother. During the active investigation, I'd fought hard for entry onto the Georges River Task Force team, annoyed and confused as to why I was being kept away from what was possibly the nation's most important case. I had the skills. I had the enthusiasm. I'd had no idea that I was being shut out because the main suspect was Sam. I'd always hated Nigel anyway, had got into a few fistfights with him in the past.

"What's the word?" I asked.

"Mr. Woolfmyer's going to be fine. He's got a mild concussion."

"Is he going to go for an assault charge?"

"Of course he is," Nigel snorted. "You knocked him out cold."

"Woolfmyer, the lawyer?" the girl on the ground broke in. "You punched a lawyer?"

I turned toward Nigel and tried to signal that my conversation with him wasn't for public consumption. But the other women in the holding cell were watching me with interest now.

"If they're going to lock me up, I want my notes on Sam's case," I said. "They're in my handbag. I'll still be able to work on his defense."

"Harry." Nigel shifted closer to the bars. "Your brother is a killer. You're going to have to move past the denial phase and wake up to what's happening here. I know you and I have had our differences. But we didn't lock him up to spite you. We locked him up because he murdered three girls."

I grabbed a handful of the magazines from the stack beside me and hurled them at the bars. Nigel flinched. The girls in the cell around me cheered. I was shocked by the noise, brought suddenly out of my fury. I realized my jaw was clenched so tight that my teeth were clicking as they ground together.

"I reckon you forced that confession out of him," I told Nigel, giving my fellow inmates a warning look. "There was a lot of pressure to catch the killer."

Nigel shook his head. "Harry, you and Sam are violent people. I've experienced your family's violence personally." He touched his brow, an old scar I'd given him about the seventh or eighth time he'd parked in my designated spot.

The girl on the floor had shifted closer to me, her grin spread wide.

"Wait a minute," she chirped up. "You mean, you punched this guy, too?" she said, flicking her chin at my colleague.

"I did," I said. I looked at Nigel. "And he cried like a baby."

CHAPTER 7

I WAS TEACHING the women in the cell how to land a left hook without fracturing their wrists when I noticed Pops standing at the door, waiting for the guard to unlock it.

My chief. My friend. My boxing trainer, a man who'd also seen the hair-trigger aggression that thrived in the very marrow of my bones. Pops said nothing as we walked down the sterile hall toward the offices. I tottered on my ridiculous heels. Eventually I stopped, reached down and pulled them off. We were standing between the row of holding cells and the doors to the bullpen where my colleagues worked, a corridor between two worlds. My brother existed in the world we'd just walked through, the criminal world. My own life, until then, had been ahead of us, in the swirling blue universe of police and their struggle against evildoers. Here I was, balancing on the tightrope connecting the two.

"I had a private chat with Judge Steiner," Pops said. "We went ahead and held the assault hearing in your absence."

"What?" I said. Suddenly, I could hardly find words, which was unusual for me.

"Woolfmyer agreed not to push forward with an assault conviction, but he applied for an AVO, and Steiner granted it."

Still no words came.

Pops raised his bushy eyebrows. "Yeah. You're banned from the trial. You're banned from the entire court-house, in fact. You're not allowed to come within five hundred meters of Prosecutor Woolfmyer. Which means anywhere he regularly goes is off limits to you. The prison where your brother is, for example. Sam's lawyer's office."

"This is . . ." I was shivering with rage.

"This is perfectly reasonable." Pops shrugged, angry. "Judge Steiner could have recorded the conviction *and* granted Woolfmyer the apprehended violence order. But he didn't. Because I convinced him you were going to get your arse out of town."

A young probationary constable was walking up the hall with my handbag, confiscated from me when I was arrested. I snatched the stupid pink bag off him and started rummaging through it for cigarettes.

"I told Steiner I'd find you a case. Send you off into the desert again for a couple of weeks so you can cool down."

"I'm not going back out there," I snapped. "I'm going to sit on the front steps of the courthouse. If I can't go inside, I'll still be there. I'm not leaving Sam."

"That's exactly what Judge Steiner said you'd do." Pops shook his head. "He wanted to lock you up instead. I said you're not going to be on the courthouse steps. You'll be out in the desert, out of trouble, just like you were after they picked Sam up."

"Nope," I said. "Not happening."

I couldn't find my cigarettes. My hands were shaking too badly.

"Blue," Pops called as I walked toward the door, following at my heels. "This is not up for discussion. You get out of here or he'll reverse his decision. And then you'll be no good to Sam at all. You want to try working on his defense from a jail cell? You'll be lucky if they give you paper and a pencil in there."

I stopped by the big glass doors.

There was a certain appeal to what he was saying. I could go back out into the Australian badlands, out among the tiny towns where people who didn't want to be recognized fled. I could run away from the horror of my brother's situation. Blessed denial.

"When does the order expire?"

"Nine days."

I bit my lip. I wanted so badly to cry. But I was not a crier. I was not weak. I squeezed the door handle, trying to hold on to some semblance of control.

"You fucked up, Blue," Pops said. It was rare that he swore. I looked at his eyes. "You're a hothead. And I love that about you. It's half of what makes you a good cop. Your fearlessness. Your fire. But you need to get away from here before you do some real damage. This?" He flipped the frilly collar of my blouse. "This is not working. When you're not bashing prosecutors you're standing around pissed as hell and doing a bad job hiding it. The princess getup makes you look about as harmless as a hired assassin."

I exhaled. I wanted a hug. But I was not a hugger, either.

"It's only nine days," he said. "How bad could things go in that time?"

CHAPTER 8

I LEANED MY head against the car window in the dark.

Beyond the glass, New South Wales desert rolled by, barren and hard. I was out here again. In exile for my own good, for the good of Sam's case.

I was six hours from Sydney, four of them by plane, two of them by car, on the straight edge of the western border of New South Wales. Red dirt country. We were headed to a tiny, dim star in a constellation of sparse towns, most notably White Cliffs to the south of us (population 103) and Tibooburra to the west of us (population 262). My driver, a plump and pretty blonde woman wearing a dusty police uniform and standard-issue baseball cap, shifted uncomfortably behind the wheel. She'd been jibber-jabbering since we left the airstrip, about the region, its history, seasonal precautions about snakes. I was so angry at myself, so distracted, I'd hardly been answering her. I sighed quietly. She was gearing up to take a run at me about why I was there. How could I possibly explain what I'd done? I could feel it—the curiosity.

"So the papers said..." She licked her lips, hesitated,

as most people do. "They said that the lawyer made some derogatory remark toward you?"

"My brother," I answered. "He made a joke about my brother being raped in prison. I work in Sex Crimes. Rape jokes aren't funny."

"Struth! You're right, they're not. Plus, it's your brother," the cop sympathized. "I mean, it doesn't matter what he did. He's still—"

"He didn't do anything. He's innocent," I said.

I realized miserably that I didn't even know this officer's name. My mind was so tangled up in my personal life that I'd completely forgotten it as soon as she'd introduced herself. I reached down for the case file at my feet and pretended I was shifting it to the backseat so it wouldn't get damaged. I glanced at the name on the cover. Senior Sergeant Victoria Snale.

"I've got to say"—Snale's voice was irrepressibly cheerful—"it made an amazing picture for the front pages. You standing over the lawyer. Him all splayed out on the concrete. It must have really been some punch."

I felt microscopically uplifted. "It doesn't have to be hard if it's on target."

"And now you're here," she said brightly. "I can't say I'm sad about that. It's pretty lonely out here, to be honest. It'll be good to have some more cops around. Someone who can relate. You know?"

"How many cops are there in town?" I asked.

"Active officers? I mean, we have one retiree..."

"Active officers."

"Just me." She looked over, smiled. "Just *us*."

I didn't want to burst Snale's bubble, but I didn't plan on being out in the desert long. *Nine days* of "us." Then it'd be back to Victoria Snale: Lone Ranger.

The moment Prosecutor Woolfmyer's AVO expired, I'd be back—back in that jerk's face, fighting him and the state's crack team of lawyers about my brother's innocence.

The empty desert around me was familiar. I'd been shoved aside when Sam had first been arrested, shipped out into the middle of nowhere, away from the public eye, away from my distinctly uncomfortable colleagues and their guilty looks after months of lying to me. Back then, I'd succumbed to the journey. I'd felt such shameful pleasure at having something to think about that was not Sam and what he was facing. Now was no different.

I squeezed my folder of notes on Sam's case against my chest. A thick binder of papers detailing all the leads I'd tried to chase down. Most of the work I'd done was hopeless, dead ends I'd pursued over the months searching for something, anything, that might set my brother free. The binder was battered and bruised, but it was my lifeline. I wasn't leaving it behind. I wasn't putting it in my bag. I was hanging on to it. As long as I had the binder, I wasn't abandoning Sam.

CHAPTER 9

"LET'S CHECK OUT the view before we go down," Victoria Snale said, beaming. "You'll love it."

The officer pulled the four-wheel drive off the side of the highway and let it rumble to a stop. I climbed out and breathed the desert air, felt the warm wind ruffle my hair. The great domed sky was heavy with stars. I felt so far from where I belonged. Wonderfully small.

"Come this way," Snale beckoned me, kicking up dust in the car's headlights. "This is it."

I stood with her on the edge of a rocky cliff in the dark. "This is Last Chance Valley," she said.

She swept her hand dramatically across the landscape, indicating a less-than-impressive collection of gold lights clustered at the bottom of a moonlit rise. I nodded, made an interested noise. I felt bad for being so distant for the whole trip toward the town.

"You can't see it very well right now, but the town is actually at the bottom of a massive crater." She pointed to the curve of the rise we stood on. "Biggest crater in the Southern Hemisphere. This ridge is just the edge, it runs all the way around. It's sort of egg-shaped, with the town right in the center and properties spreading out around. The first family settled down there two hundred years ago. There are seventy-five residents now."

"Uh-huh."

"They're not sure what formed the crater, but it may have been a volcano. A meteorite. Every now and then somebody comes out and runs a study on the place. Very exciting stuff. I usually get to brief the town on their visits, tell everybody to behave themselves."

"Sounds great."

"I guess the settlers thought the crater might shelter us from the desert dust storms," she mused, rolling a rock under her boot. "It doesn't. In fact it makes things worse. We get about ten centimeters of dust when the summer winds roll in. It also floods real bad, and the floodwaters hold beneath the earth. When it floods, we get green grass. We can grow wheat here. There's plenty of cattle. But, being the only grass around for thousands and thousands of kilometers, it brings locust plagues."

I was glad Snale was the local cop and not the tourism director. I tried to maintain a serious face.

"Locusts?" I said.

"Yeah, we're just getting over the last plague. Here's one right now, in fact."

She reached out toward me, and I realized a creature was walking up my biceps, an enormous brown grasshopper covered in the patterns of the desert, spots and stripes in red and brown. I didn't scream. But it wasn't easy.

Snale plucked the creature from my shirt and tossed it into the wind. It fluttered into the dark.

"Oh great," I said, brushing off the place where the thing had been. "This is great."

"They bite, but it's not that painful."

"And what exactly will I be working on out here?" I asked.

"Well," she said cheerfully. "Turns out somebody's planning to kill us all."

CHAPTER 10

WE SAT IN the car together and Snale took a package from the glove compartment. It was a notebook secured in a police evidence bag, a sheaf of photocopies, which she handed to me. She started the car but kept the overhead light on so I could read as she drove.

"A trucker found this diary in a backpack on the side of this highway, at a rest stop." She pointed over her shoulder. "Back the way we came, about five kilometers. He spotted it sitting there when he stopped to pull a dead roo from his front grille. Brought the diary into town and handed it in to me. It contains detailed analyses of spree killers, weapons, massacre plans. We think someone is, or was, constructing a plan to kill as many people in Last Chance Valley as possible."

"When was this?"

"Two days ago."

"And you vetted the truck driver?"

"Yeah, I let him go."

I felt the hairs on the back of my neck stand on end as I looked at the photocopied pages before me. My eyes breezed over the tight, small writing and fell upon the hand-drawn images, sketches of a person in a hood running toward fleeing groups of people, mowing them down with a huge rifle. There were diagrams of the layout of the town below, lists of names and addresses. I examined the notebook in the evidence bag, turned it over. Of course, there was no name on it. That'd be too much to hope for.

The thing that struck me immediately about the pages I was looking through was the sheer weight of preparation that the diarist had gone to. Every page was filled on both sides with either illustrations or notes, or with excerpts from books that had been copied and pasted onto some pages. It was all very calm and methodical. Where there were illustrations, they were very well done. More like scenes of war than the macabre scribblings of a maniac. There were photographs of buildings, I assumed areas of the tiny town below us from different angles. This was more than a speculative work. This was serious.

Snale drove us over the edge of the crater and down toward its depths. I looked up at the other edge of the valley, rocky and pointed against the burnt-orange light.

And as I looked across the crater I saw the explosion.

The sound it made took seconds to reach us across the distance. A bass thump I felt in the center of my chest.

The sky lit up with a fireball directly across from us, on the steep rise.

"Oh my God!" Snale swerved, gripping the wheel.

I shoved the papers aside and sat bolt upright. "Get there. Get there *now!*"

CHAPTER 11

THE EXPLOSION ON the other side of the town seemed to have ignited the brush there in flames. I kept my eyes on the dim glow as we raced up the main street and between the fields beyond. Small houses. Fences. Snale's jaw was set. She squinted at the dark rise before us.

"Might have been kids with fireworks," she murmured. "The kids around here, they're pretty feral."

"Those are some pretty big fireworks," I said.

We took the winding road up the slope at a roaring pace. I gripped the door of the vehicle as Snale took the corners. Country driver. She'd been taking these roads at breakneck speed since girlhood.

We could smell the blast zone from the side of the road as we parked. Snale was no athlete but she bounded into the bush ahead of me, agile as a rabbit, her gun drawn. I had no flashlight, but followed the bouncing white light of hers, razor-sharp desert plants slicing at my jeans. The fire was burning itself out in the tough grass and the oily leaves of the eucalypts above us.

The smoke seared my eyes. We split up. I almost

tripped over a plastic chair, or what remained of it. Three of its metal legs were buried in the dirt, and the back had melted to a black husk, sharp, sticking upwards like a dagger. Snale came back to me, huffing, winding her flashlight beam across my face, then to where I was crouched, examining the chair.

"May I?" I grabbed the light and swept it over the chair, found the crater where the bomb had gone off. There were bodily remains here, tangled in the dirt and grass. The blackened and burned slivers of flesh of something or someone blown to bits.

"Oh no," Snale was saying gently, following close behind me. "Oh no. Oh no."

I zeroed in on a shiny object—a hand wheel valve. There were splinters of metal shining in the dust. Entrails, blood everywhere. Hair. An animal? I nudged the valve with my boot, didn't have evidence bags with me.

"Propane gas bottle," I said.

"Oh man." Snale gave a frightened shudder, taking the light from me with her cold fingers. "Oh maaaaan!"

I followed her. She'd noticed something hanging from a nearby branch, swinging gently in the breeze. It was a man's hand and forearm, blackened and charred, held there by the remains of a shred of melted duct tape. The tape wrapped around the wrist seemed burned to the flesh.

I was just beginning to wonder how on earth it was still hanging on when it fell, slapping to the ground at our feet. Snale yelped in terror. She grabbed at me as a new fear rushed through her: the sound of a large vehicle leaving the roadside back near where we'd parked.

We could hear it crashing through the undergrowth toward us.

CHAPTER 12

DEER-HUNTING LIGHTS. Eight of them. They pierced the night around us, blasting through my vision, making me cower behind my arm. It was like an alien ship landing. Snale cocked her weapon, but in seconds she seemed to relax.

"Oh. It's only Kash," she said. There was a slight upward lilt to her voice, like she'd just been given good news. I was still blinded. I stumbled forward, grabbing the back of her shirt to guide me through the painfully illuminated blast zone.

"Jesus, those lights!"

"Hands up!" someone bellowed. "Identify yourselves!"

"It's me!" Snale put her hands up. I didn't bother. "It's us. Vicky, and my new friend Harriet."

I thought "friend" was going a bit far.

An enormous man emerged out of the light like an overexcited dog, a flurry of hard breath and wild gesturing. Incredibly, he had a flashlight in his hand.

"Vicky. Right. Have you seen the suspect? Where's the suspect? Any signs of where he went?"

"The what?" I tried to see his face, glimpsing a chiseled jaw, black curls. "What suspect?"

"You"—Kash pointed at me—"head down the hill and sweep south-east in a standard second-leg search pattern. Snale and I will take southwest. Give it a K, maybe a K and a half. We'll meet back here in twenty."

"A search?" I yelled. "Using what? I'm not sure I'll ever see again."

"Double time! Let's go!"

The muscled goliath took off into the bush, crashing over plants and shrubs like a tank. I jogged, confused, in the general direction he'd indicated.

There was nothing to indicate that a suspect was on the loose. But the big man in the dark had overcome my decision-making abilities with his barking voice, like a slap to the side of the head. I was annoyed and bristled, but I did what he said. There was no one south or east of the blast zone.

Snale and the big man, Kash, were there when I returned. She was searching the remains again with her flashlight beam. Kash was standing uselessly with his hands on his hips, looking generally "in charge" of whatever might have been about to happen. In the light of the enormous truck I saw an action-figure body and Clark Kent glasses on a head as square and thick as a sandstone block. When I came back into the light, he walked toward me, hand extended.

"Elliot Kash, Counter-Terrorism Task Force, Islamic Fundamentalism Division, ASIO."

"Of course." I nodded. I understood all the dramatics now. This guy was in national security. I'd come across his type before. "Of course you are."

"You've heard of me then? Good. That'll save time. Let's secure the entry to the blast zone, erect a checkpoint on the road. We'll do hourly sweeps of the search grid to see if the suspect comes back. They often return to film their work for their online campaigns."

I noticed Kash hadn't asked me for my name, or a long-winded explanation of my position within the police. I let it go.

"Who exactly are you talking about?" I asked. "We've got a dead guy and a bomb. How do you know who else was involved?"

"You've seen the diary?"

"Barely," I said.

"Well, you're behind." Kash sighed. "You can get a de-briefing once we've established a secure boundary. We need to act now and ask questions later. Get going. I'll take charge here."

I suffered the same verbal slap to the head, the phenom-enon of compliance sweeping over me like a spell. I found myself walking back toward the road, thinking I'd move Snale's truck, put lights on the road, see if she had some traffic cones in the back to guide any passersby onto the shoulder so we could question them. I didn't further an-alyze Kash's resolve that a dangerous suspect was behind this, and that it was possible he or she was somewhere around here.

The spell wore off before I hit the roadside. I stopped, frowned, tried to get my thoughts in order. Snale bumped into me from behind. She'd been jogging up the path behind me.

"Sorry." She sniffed. "I've got to get to the radio and call in the team from the next town over. We need more people. This is bad. This is really bad."

"It's OK." I jogged alongside her. This was probably the most terrible crime to ever happen in Last Chance Valley. Maybe the only serious crime they'd ever had. "Agent Dickhead's got it all under control."

"You don't understand," she said. "I just found the victim's head. I know who he is. He's my chief."

CHAPTER 13

HE CAME EVERY second night when the temperature began to sink, at what Caitlyn assumed was sunset outside her concrete room. The first few times, she tried to brace herself for what was about to happen. She visualized it for hours on end, her skin crawling and stomach turning, trying to decide how she would endure the rape or torture or prolonged death he had planned for her. But after a week, when none of those things had happened, a deep, sickening confusion set in. And then there was the rage. Caitlyn sat on the mattress in the dark and boiled with a quiet, dangerous rage.

The man with the shaved head came and unlocked the door, walked down the steps and put her supplies on the floor. Two packaged sandwiches, one chicken and one roast beef, the kind a person buys at the service station. Two bottles of water. Two chocolate bars. One roll of toilet paper for the bucket in the corner. He wouldn't look at her. The ritual was always the same. He came, he dropped the supplies, he changed the bucket, and he left, locking the door securely behind him.

Caitlyn had tried everything she could think of. She'd waited by the door and swung a wine bottle she'd found in the crates at his head, missed her target by centimeters. The wine was expired and tasted foul, but after breaking a couple of bottles she'd come up with a good, shiny dagger that she came at him with the next time, again to no avail. He'd shoved her hard down the stairs, and she'd lain crying, the back of her head bleeding on the cold stone floor.

The next time, she'd been a bit trickier. Caitlyn had pulled lengths of fabric from the old mattress and woven them into a strong trip-wire, pulled this across the doorway. He'd tripped, and she'd launched herself at him, clubbed him hard in the back of the skull with a lump of wood broken from one of the crates. She'd got through the doorway and looked down the dark hall that led to wherever she was before he'd grabbed her ankle and dragged her back into her prison room. Down the hall she'd seen a long concrete walkway, stairs to the upper levels, and plenty more heavy trash that he dragged in front of the door after he locked it. Caitlyn glimpsed flyers on the ground, warped and yellowed, a box of molded brass numbers, the kind a person would screw to a door or the front of a house. An old hotel? The power must still be turned on for her television to work. Why couldn't anyone hear her cries? Was she underground?

Caitlyn didn't know if her captor was just unusually strong or if the rations and the lack of sleep had left her weak. She was no match for him. As the days passed, it became harder for her to wake. Harder to think. Harder to cry. In the daytime, she screamed for help. At night she sat and watched the television in the corner, pulling at strands of her hair.

Caitlyn recognized this for what it was. A holding pattern. Something had gone wrong with his plan, whatever it had been. Now he was simply keeping her alive. Uninterested. Out of ideas. If he didn't want sex from her, and he didn't want to torture her, and he didn't want to talk to her, why the hell was he doing this?

When the news came on, it was more often than not about the Georges River Killer's arrest. Sam Blue had featured in the media for months.

She sat chewing her nails and remembering the first night in the concrete bunker, one of the only times she'd seen her captor show overt emotion. Surprise and rage at the image of Samuel Blue on the screen. He'd said it wasn't finished yet. That this wasn't the plan.

What wasn't the plan? Caitlyn knew she hadn't been her captor's planned victim. That the girl she'd interrupted him trying to abduct had been the one who was supposed to be here now. But was it more than that? Caitlyn remembered the man standing before the television screen, running his fingers up the back of his skull, gripping at the muscles in his neck as they locked, rock hard, with anger. Sam Blue's arrest. Did that have something to do with it all?

Was this man the Georges River Killer's partner?

CHAPTER 14

EDWARD WHITTACKER STRAIGHTENED his tie in his reflection in the courthouse windows, smoothed down a cowlick at the side of his narrow head. He felt strangely lonely without Harriet, although she'd been so detached since the beginning of the Blue hearings that sometimes he'd forgotten she was there beside him, fidgeting in her "pretty sister" getup.

She'd been impossible to talk to in the weeks since their return from the desert, when Whitt decided he'd leave his home in Perth and come to Sydney to support the new partner he'd learned to admire. She was a hard creature, Harriet Blue. Unpredictable and sharp edged. When he'd met her on their case in Western Australia, her brother had just been arrested, and she'd been stripped bare of the minimal friendliness she managed to maintain in order to get on with others. But in their time in the Outback, fleeing a sniper who was hunting young men and women like dogs, the Sex Crimes detective had grown on him. She was a good person, even if that goodness was buried deep under plenty of bad behavior. He wanted to help her. And now that she'd gone and got herself banished from the courthouse altogether, he had no choice but to be her representative. It was what good friends did.

Whitt now stood watching at the edge of the crowd gathered around the New South Wales Police Commissioner on the courthouse steps, a tall, broad man wearing a uniform laden in red and silver buckles and stars. Microphones bobbed and swayed as Commissioner Sorrell moved his head. A petite journalist at the front of the crowd was trying not to be pressed against the man by the bigger journalists behind her shoving forward to catch quotes.

"We have faith that Caitlyn McBeal will be located safe and well," Sorrell said. "We know that she has not fallen victim to the Georges River Killer, because our primary suspect in that case was under surveillance the entire day she disappeared. At the approximate time of Caitlyn's last confirmed sighting four months ago, Sydney police detectives already had Samuel Jacob Blue in custody. That's all I can say right now."

Whitt knew some of the inside information about the Caitlyn McBeal abduction. The supposed incident at the University of Sydney hadn't even made the news right away. Television screens across the country had been flooded with images of Sam Blue's arrest from that morning. But way down the list of items on online news sites, a vague story was emerging. A young student from the university, Linny Simpson, was claiming someone had tried to abduct her from a car park and she'd managed to escape, passing an African American girl as she ran to safety. That African American girl fit the description of the now-missing Caitlyn McBeal.

Whitt had been exhilarated. Was this the Georges River Killer, trying to nab another victim only hours after Sam had been arrested? If it was, then surely Sam would go free! The nightmare for his friend and her brother would be over. All they had to do was find Caitlyn McBeal.

Then problems started to emerge with Linny and her tale. Linny admitted she'd fainted after reaching the bottom of the stairs of the car park, terrified by her ordeal. She'd hit her head and suffered a concussion. Details of her ordeal were inconsistent across her interviews with police. Her abductor had tried to get her into a white van. No, a green van. He'd been tall. Maybe not so tall. There had been another girl in the car park. Caitlyn and one other. Two others, maybe.

Then Linny's history was exposed. Her teenage drug use. A stalking report against an ex-boyfriend that had been entered and then withdrawn. The police were still searching for Caitlyn McBeal, and were heartened by reported sightings of her in Queensland. Maybe she'd just run off. That was the solution in most Missing Persons cases. The stress and struggle of daily life simply got too much. They dropped their belongings and fled, started again somewhere new. Whitt had seen it plenty of times during his career. He'd seen mothers lock the front door on their children and simply wander off, turning up years later with a new name, a new job, halfway across the country. Caitlyn was young and alone on the opposite side of the planet from her life back home. She had no serious commitments. Disappearing, even just for a while, would be easy.

Whatever had happened to Caitlyn, Linny Simpson's explanation for it wasn't anyone's favorite lead, because she was inconsistent. Confused.

But if she was right, even somewhere *close* to the truth, it meant two things that no one on the Georges River case wanted to admit.

That Sam Blue was innocent.

And that the killer was still out there.

CHAPTER 15

I STOOD BY the side of the road, watching the sun rising on the distant edge of the crater, a depthless black in silhouette against warm pink. The temperature was coming up fast. Soon the town below me would be swirling with gossip about the explosion in the early hours. Already, local farmers who had heard the bang and become curious had started to line the roadside, eyeing me cautiously as they met with Snale to get the lowdown.

The town's only police officer was barely keeping it together. Snale's chief, a man in his sixties named Theo "Soupy' Campbell, owned the bloodied, dirt-clodded head she had found about ten meters from the center of the blast zone. I assumed he'd owned the arm we'd seen hanging from the tree, and the various other bits and pieces of human that had been strewn about the bush. We hadn't done too much more wandering around in the crime scene. It was best to leave it for Forensics, who would soon be boarding a helicopter back in Sydney. The entire police force from the nearest town, Milparinka, were on their way to help us secure the scene and the dead police chief's truck, which we'd found parked in the bush on the opposite side of the road to the blast. Milparinka's force comprised two officers, bringing our total to five. I felt drastically out of my depth. I was used to securing crime scenes with the help of dozens of people, patrollies covering doorways with tape, chiefs standing about looking important before the cameras, forensics experts donning their gear.

I went to Snale's truck and sat in the front passenger seat with the door open, brought out the photocopy of the diary and began reading through it again. I didn't want to leap to any conclusions about the connection of the bomb to the book. Yes, what had happened to Chief Campbell looked like murder. The duct tape on the wrist was a sure sign, even if one accepted the highly improbable idea that he'd chosen to commit suicide by bomb when he likely had a perfectly good gun in his possession. I needed to find something in the diary that connected the idea and the crime.

The first pages were all about guns. I spread a page over my knee and looked at the photocopied pictures of two handsome teenage boys.

The page was a study of the Columbine killers, Eric Harris and Dylan Klebold, who'd gone on a shooting spree at their local high school in Colorado, killing twelve students and a teacher and injuring twenty-four others. I knew the story, had read a couple of true crime books about it. The diarist had made a list, beside a doodled sketch of the wolfish Harris, entitled "Successes."

1. Kept the circle of conspirators small.
2. Surveillance of victims for maximum impact.
3. Covert weapons purchases.

What was this? A list of the things the Columbine killers had done right in their evil plan? Was the diarist comparing and contrasting the massacre plans of high-profile shooters to come up with the perfect kill plot? I flipped the page. More about the Columbine killers' work, excerpts from the boys' diaries and maps of their school. There were five pages dedicated to the Columbine shooting in the diary. A sickly feeling was creeping up from the pit of my stomach. I ran my fingers over a note at the bottom of the last page on Columbine.

Thirteen victims, it read. *I can beat that!*